ROTTEN
TO
THE
CORE

Why Politicians and Other Humans Are What They Are

CONTENTS

PERSPECTIVE & CONTEXT

Before getting into the substance of this book, I'll introduce myself in order that you have an idea of the lens through which I observe the universe. I have always found it helpful to understand the prejudices and the agenda of the author while reading. I immediately state right off that I have very few prejudices but I do have an agenda: to bring our human, ingrained and perpetual evil traits to your conscious level.

I have little formal education and training in the field for which this book is written. However, I am not entirely without education, training or experience. My education includes a Bachelor of Science degree in economics, a Master's degree in education and a Juris Doctor degree; I have practiced law for nearly 40 years.

I have worked since I was 14 years old and am now in my mid 70s. I've been in about 40 of our states and in over 10 countries. I served in the U.S. Navy both as enlisted and as an officer. I've worked in two large sheriff's offices, a district attorney's office, have been the first on the scene of more violent deaths than I'll ever talk about and try not to think about. I've taught (part time) in three colleges and have been a guest lecturer in more places than I can recall – including the FBI Academy. I've also had more articles published than I can recite and have been quoted in at least one history book.

The subject matter of this book is a topic which I have discussed with professionals in the various fields discussed. I have also spent countless hours of research on the topics covered and have read a great deal of history. Mostly I rely on my own and my friends' common sense and everyday observations of life – observations of the human species.

INTRODUCTION

We humans are unique for that the evil we do. While we have the imagination to create and carry out grotesquely evil deeds on a grand scale, we also have the intelligence to keep those drives in check – we simply choose not to do so. We have continuously brought devastation down on both individuals and nations.

The root cause of the evil we do is our selfish attitude that the universe is all about me; that there is nothing more important than ourselves. We have now taken self indulgence to a new level – the demand for immediate gratification. The line between need and want has become blurred. As to everything in life, we need/want/deserve it now!

Do not look for a solution in this book – there is none; at least not for the human species overall. Each individual may however, if they choose, exert self-discipline to live a life without the self-indulgence discussed in this book.

This topic has been buzzing around in my head for decades. I've spoken with many friends and acquaintances about the topic of why are we (humans) the way we are. Why can't we be better individually and as a society? We certainly see our own and societies' shortfalls. We understand that we could do better. But we just keep making the same mistakes over and over.

Take crime for instance. We all (including the criminals) know what we should and should not do. We all (except the small number of truly mentally deranged) have the ability to make better decisions about our conduct. Even though we have this knowledge and ability, we, as a species, continue to have a substantial percentage of our population committing crimes.

Criminal activity has always been with us. However, in all my years, I keep seeing politicians, bureaucrats and touchy-feely do-gooders asking for more and more tax dollars to fund their wonderful new (meaning a new name on some old failed theory) programs which will end criminal activity. You cannot go back in the history of any society where you will not find crime, torture, and countless accounts of man's inhumanity to man.

I did read an article a long time ago that claimed that there was no evidence of crime among the Australian Aboriginals and the Alaskan Eskimos before the coming of the Europeans. This was claimed to be due to their native languages not having a word for (nor concept of) "disobedience." I don't know if that's true, but I add that to be completely honest as to what I have read.

Of course I've also read early accounts of how the Eskimos were among the most sophisticated ever at torture and they preferred the Russians to the English and French because the Russians lasted longer under torture.

Much of what you will find in this book refers us to the animal kingdom for examples. For the few of you who haven't heard the news (or deny it) we humans are animals and have much of the same basic behavioral patterns as all the rest of those animals with which we share this planet. They need nourishment, shelter and propagate – just like we do.

The reference to "politicians" in the title is because I find that as a particular demographic, they do not use the human ability of volition to avoid the basic animal behaviors which will be discussed in the pages that follow. I have managed political campaigns, had closed door planning sessions which included governors and U.S. Senators among others. I have heard them laugh about the very citizens they serve and depend upon for re-election calling them "The Great Unwashed" among other derogatory names. Sadly, when I was in my late 20s and active with these people, I did the same.

CHAPTER I

I, ME, MY

"COGITO ERGO SUM" "I think, therefore I am." Rene Descartes (1596 – 1650). This is his most famous quote. He was a French philosopher and mathematician. He is considered the Father of Modern Philosophy and also the Father of Analytical Geometry.

Perhaps even more basic than "I think, therefore I am." is the attitude that each of us is the absolute center of the universe. The "universe" (meaning *everything*) is *all* about ME! Some people think "The Holy Trinity" is: Me, Myself and I.

Think about it for a few minutes: If you never existed, then to you, what would the universe, your most beloved person or your dearest memory be. NOTHING! NOTHING! Not even numb blackness – for even numb blackness would be something that you sensed. Had you never existed you wouldn't even have a concept of

NOTHINGNESS. You certainly would not be reading this book.

The I, Me, My attitude is natural. The only things that exist for you are those things which you perceive through one or more of your senses. But, you say, what about those things which I never knew of and now I have become aware of them. They existed before, even though I didn't know they were there. You're correct, however, it would have mattered not to you had you not made the discovery – they may as well never existed. Absolutely nothing has any conscience significance to you until you sense its existence.

Therefore, as just mentioned, the I, Me, My attitude is in fact normal and natural. Since none of all that out there exists except through me, then I am the center of the universe – not the geographic or astronomical center, but the sensory center of the universe. It is then *all* about ME!

We'll leave the intellectual theory aside and get down to the base element of this chapter's topic by first turning to the animal kingdom – the non-human animal kingdom.

If you think that you'll not find "it's all about me" in the animal kingdom, just try to take a meaty bone from a hungry Pit Bull! It shouldn't take much thought for you to get the feeling of "it's all about me" with that picture in your mind. "It's all about me" for you and the Pit Bull: the Pit Bull needs to eat to survive and you need to leave him alone so you can survive.

Think again of the National Geographic and other wildlife documentaries we've seen along with portions of various movies. In the animal kingdom we always find a form of dominance hierarchy. This hierarchy will be either a linear ranking – what we often call a "pecking order" or a despotic system where there is one dominant leader and all the rest are equally submissive.

"Alpha Male" is a term familiar to almost everybody. The Alpha Male is the one which is dominant over all the others of the group regardless of if the system is linear or despotic. This individual animal will use threats, aggression, dominance displays and outright fighting to maintain his position. As he ages and younger ones become stronger, he will eventually be replaced.

While each Alpha Male is at the top, he will have the most and the choicest foods, choice of mates and the most space within the group's territory. It's all about him and he will not give it up easily to the next who thinks it is all about him – the new, younger stronger him.

You will see this territorial "it's all about me" among domestic animals also. We use nice P.C. terms for the process such as "spraying" or "marking their territory." What they are doing is letting other animals that come into the area know that this is their territory – it's all about me.

Domestic pet owners know very well about animal's "it's all about me" personality traits – and those pet owners accommodate them. The dog – or whatever – wants attention, to be loved, petted, fed, etc. The pet owner can't wait to do just what the pet wants – even to neglecting members of their own family. Oh, excuse me; the pet is a member of the family.

Nature seems to have a hand in helping the males in the animal kingdom with the "I, Me, My" also. Take a look throughout the animal kingdom. Which of the genders is the most colorful, largest and loudest – the males. The most obvious example we all have seen is the Peacock – larger and much more colorful than the Peahen. Much of this has to do with the prior chapter's theme of survival of the species.

We've briefly thought about it above in the animal kingdom, but it's so natural it's even present in plants. Again, think of the nature documentaries you've seen. How many flowering plants have you seen with amazing displays to attract bees and other bugs to spread their pollen? We've even seen plants that are carnivorous that are disguised as something else then eat the bugs that land on them. Even at this level we have survival that is "all about me."

As we did in the previous chapter, now that we've considered our animal friends, let's take a look at us humans. Recall now, that humans have this great intellect – IQs that leave the animals way, way in the back of the class. We have all that nice big cerebral cortex that allows us to really think about our actions – to consider consequences, an imagination, self control and not to just act on our urges.

So let's consider just what we do with all that brain power.

That we humans have this "it's all about me" predisposition in us is completely natural as stated earlier. In getting to us humans, let's just do a quick little list of the words in the chapter title: "I, Me, My."

I went to Hawaii on my vacation.
I went skydiving.
I made the best apple pie.
I have the hottest car of all my friends.
I am a member of the Chamber of Commerce.
I am on the Board of Directors of.............
I bought a new suit.
I have six of those at home.
I ran a marathon.
I lost 20 pounds.

Take Me to the store.
Come to Me.
That dress makes Me look heavy.
The bright red car belongs go Me.
Include Me.
What about Me?
Of course he loves Me.
If it were up to Me,.....
They can't get along without Me.
Hey, look at Me.

My kids.
My opinion.
My house.
My church.
My family.

My car.
My country.
My suit.
My team.
My friends.

Did any of those sound familiar? Could you go an entire day without using any of the words: "I, Me, My"? It's difficult to even get through a single conversation without using one of these three words. We've all known people who are more prone than others to use those words – these people are often so self-centered (concentric personalities) that they don't even realize that is how they speak and think.

We'll turn to practical examples that should be very familiar to you. In many of the following examples, you may not have thought about the self-centered personality that such activities and statements display. After reading this chapter and considering the topic, perhaps you may:

Become more aware of these selfish attitudes in others.
Become more aware of these selfish attitudes in yourself.
Change the manner in which you center everything in yourself.
Not recognize it in yourself and go on as you are.

I'll bet on the last one.

I'll list some examples of I, Me, My conduct. Of the examples, think of how many you have seen, heard or done yourself? Rank them as "Ridiculous," "Pathetic," "Socially acceptable," "That's the way it is," and "Good personality traits or good goals to live by." I'll try not to editorialize by the manner in which each is presented, at least I'll try – most of the time anyway:

(By the way, these are not presented in any particular order of any kind. The numbering is for your convenience, for whatever purpose you may have.)

1.　　The kid with the neon-green hair. I kind of feel sorry for him and others that draw attention to themselves through decorating themselves in obvious ways. In my opinion, they feel deep within themselves that they are nothing or so near nothing and that this is the only way they can feel any sort of "I, Me, My." Without such display they would be nothing at all. While often non-violent, it's easy to place them into the same family of those who go off with guns and shoot up a school, a store or randomly targets people.

2.　　"Winning isn't everything, it's the only thing." A famous pro football coach is given credit for this one, but it's likely that it started with a couple of college coaches who he paraphrased. It's the "team" equivalent of the "I, Me, My." I won. Look at Me. It's My trophy.

3.　　Photos!! How many photo studios are there? How many cameras are there? Cameras are on cell phones and other phone devices. We've got no end of "Selfies" on the internet.

How many social networks are there? Type into a search engine social networks and start looking at statistics. There are hundreds of social networks – currently dominated by "facebook" on which people spend 700 billion minutes per month according to the last statistic I read. Almost all of them have photos of themselves and their friends. How could the founder of facebook go wrong by coming up with something that capitalizes on "I, Me, My"?

When you watch the news, when you watch a sporting event, does it surprise you at all that there are so many people trying to get in front of the camera? It's all about them. Even at tragic news scenes, you'll see people trying to get their face time on TV.

4.   What were your kids' grades? My child is on the Dean's List. Who has the highest grades? It's not who helped the elderly disabled neighbor by cleaning debris out of their yard – no glory there! I got a higher score on the test than Sally!

5.   A close relative to "4" above: "It's so nice that your Larry graduated Magna Cum Laude. Did I tell you that my little Julie graduated Summa Cum Laude?" I'd like to hear that one so I could come back at them with an "Oh, did you understand that Larry received a Magna Cum Laude? Actually it was an Egregia Cum Laude." Take that and stuff it in your Depends lady!!

6.   And then there are the dog shows, horse shows and other such pet contests. If you think it's about the dogs, cats, horses and parrots, you're really kidding

yourselves. It's all about the owners and trainers – the owners more than the trainers. If you haven't seen it, buy or rent the movie "Best in Show." It's about a dog show and it's a kick.

7.   One of the saddest examples: little kid sports and other contests. Parents dressing and making up their little 4 to 6 year old little girls like something out of an X rated movie. I'm not for a loss for words as to what I think of those parents when I'm in a private discussion but I'll not elaborate here. I'll only say that utter disgust is way too mild a phrase.

Similarly but only slightly less appalling are the parents that live vicariously through their kids in youth sports. I'm not necessarily talking about high school sports although you'll see some of this to a lesser degree with high school sports, but I'm discussing the pre-high school sports.

Consider little boys from age about 6 and up playing football in full gear – helmet, shoulder pads and other uniform equipment. How often do you see the parents – almost always the dads – beet read in the face screaming at their little boy who's out there doing his best while confused about the entire process? When that dad isn't screaming at his son he's screaming at the official – often a volunteer who's there to help the kids learn and keep them safe – or screaming at the coach about how he's calling the plays. I guess utter disgust would be fitting here for my opinion of these dads.

I've coached youth football and I want to make it clear that there are a lot of wonderful parents, coaches and officials out there that are looking out for the kids and making sure they have a safe, fun learning experience. But we've all seen those few parents who should be subject to retroactive contraception.

8.   Sports. The word always brings to mind winners and losers. It's all about the winners. Who remembers the losers? "I won!" The Olympics: Gold, Silver and Bronze medals. The countries and individual citizens live vicariously through the individual athletes from their countries. Each athlete competes for dominance in their event. There is, for the three best performers in each event, a pecking order – remember the linear domination system? For all others it's the despotic system; the rest are all equally submissive – or equally dismissed.

Only the medal winners can claim the "I, Me, My" of the Olympics. We fans – be it the Olympics or other sports – have to swallow hard and realize that we are merely the submissive class of a despotic system. That kind of takes the fun out of wearing your team's logo on your cap, T-shirt, jacket and such.

9.   A really definite topic for "it's all about me" – Plastic Surgery. I'm not talking about the necessary reconstructive plastic surgery due to severe injury or traumatic illness. Here we're discussing the ladies that get multiple breast implants until they look like they're carrying a couple of watermelons on their chest. How about the ladies that get face lift after face lift until their

face looks like its made of smooth skin-colored plastic – I've seen a politician or two with that look.

And, let's not forget the men. How about hair implants? Men also get face lifts. I've seen some that should get face lifts. Then there's the really far out surgeries that are definitely "all about me" – whoever me may be. If that sounds odd, here we just bring up the topic of sex change surgery. OK that's enough about sex change surgery – ouch, like really, really ouch.

10.   Historically, that is before we had the entire planet mapped and borders drawn wherever people wanted to draw them – rather wherever those people who won the wars wanted to draw them – there was the age of exploration and discovery. I've heard some joke about how the aboriginals of the various continents didn't know who they were or where they were until the Europeans came and informed them. They didn't know they were lost or the name of the place they were living until they were "discovered."

How fortunate for all those people living in the western hemisphere that the Europeans came to help them and teach them how to be civilized. Who, me sarcastic? Never!

The Europeans certainly knew best. How else would they have been able to teach all those people where and how they should live? I would expect that each of those expedition leaders didn't need to seek advice and counseling on self-esteem.

11.   What if you, or some other person – you know, the other guy – is just mediocre or somewhat below. How do they get up to that "I, Me, My" level of internalized concentric personal esteem? It's something we've all seen and in this day and age and in this country, we see it all too often. Let's call it "living down."

Living down is where the subject person finds somebody lesser than themselves in the particular topic of discussion. "Well my "D" is better than Tommy's "F."" "My car may leak oil and have bald tires, but George's car doesn't run and has been in his front yard for six months." "I may be over weight, but Jennifer's so skinny she rattles when she walks."

Living down is a way to keep you comfortable with the "it's all about me" society we live in. It's so much easier than "living up" – that is working to improve yourself. Working to gain more education, searching for a better job, putting in extra time, performing at your maximum, pushing yourself, that all takes hard work – we certainly don't want to get involved in that upward spiral.

12.   A situation which leaves me with mixed (but negative) feelings about I, Me, My conduct is seen when people are in their last days of life and then at the deceased's funeral. I believe that in most cases the concern expressed for the terminally ill is all about the afflicted person. I believe the same to be true at funerals in the mourners' focus truly being on the deceased. Those are not the people we're talking about here.

However there are many people whose focus is on themselves. Listen to some of the comments carefully: "I'm going to miss him so much." "What am I going to do without her." "I'm so sad." "I feel so lost." "My world just isn't the same without him." "I'm going to be so lonesome." "I need closure." "I'm going to have to seek help to deal with her loss." "What am I going to do with that big house now that it's so empty?" "I need to be alone for a while." "I'm going to go back to all the places we visited together." "I'm going to re-decorate a room with his photos and memorabilia so I can always have him with me."

Or, if the person is in hospice – home or elsewhere: "I need to start planning for his passing." "I hate having to make the funeral arrangements." "I don't know how I'm going to pay all the bills." "I want to be with him as much as I can before he goes." And many of the expressions from the above paragraph also fit into the hospice scenario. If you talk to these people about the situation in which they find themselves – the soon to be passing or the recent passing of a loved one – they would be horribly insulted if you were to even hint that all the concern they are expressing is about themselves.

There was a story about four guys playing golf one afternoon. A funeral passed by and one of the four stopped, took off his golf cap and placed it over his heart until the funeral procession passed.

One of his buddies said: "Charlie, that was a really nice thing to do – very respectful."

Charlie replied: "It's the least I could do – we were married 40 years."

At least Charlie was honest about it.

13.   Then there are the young guys and their cars and pick-up trucks. If those bright, shiny, big wheeled, loud sound systems that register on the Richter scale, loud exhaust system vehicles aren't a testimony to "I, Me, My" "It's all about me" then nothing is. Ladies, if that's what your new male friend shows up in – run away as fast as you can.

At a luncheon I attended a long time ago, I recall a lady that was a defense attorney (who later became a judge) making a comment about guys demonstrating the I, Me, My trait; I also recall being quite shocked at the time. She said: "You know those guys with pick-up trucks with the really big wheels and tires?" The few of us that were sitting near her nodded acknowledgement, then she continued: "The size of their penises are inversely proportional to the size of the wheels on their trucks."

I told her about the little 12 inch wheels on my compact Chevrolet Sprint.

14.   There was a study done once – you can look it up; I think it was by the University of Minnesota, but it could have been some other university – the study involved complaints by employees in the work place. Regardless of where the particular company was located or the nature of the work being done, in office settings, the number one complaint was that the temperature was too

high and number two was that the temperature was too low – same work spaces. Other companies were the reverse: number one was the temperature was too low and number two was that it was too high.

The office temperature issue is one of my pet peeves regarding "I, Me, My" "It's all about me." The owner, manager or supervisor walks in to the space and immediately goes over and changes the thermostat to what they want for their comfort. Right after changing the setting they walk out of the space to his or her individual office where they have the temperature set for what they want. Up and down, up and down, whoever is going by the thermostat seems to believe that they are the ultimate authority on what the temperature should be – never mind the other hundred people in the work area.

I even see this at church. I don't know how many times different individuals will go to the thermostat and make a change to make sure that the temperature is set just right for them. What a great Christian attitude.

Heck, I even see this at home. I'll be working away at my desk and my wife comes home from whatever activity she was involved in. I'm comfortable with the heat setting as it is. She has come out of either a cool air conditioned (or heated) car and the temperature in the house doesn't match what she had going in the car – so, right to the thermostat.

15.   As long as we're talking about "I, Me, My" let's briefly talk about talking. What's the best way to carry on a conversation with somebody to whom you were

just introduced? What is the best way to make a really favorable impression on that person?

The answer to this one is simple and should, by now, be very obvious: talk about their favorite subject – them!

Actually this holds for most any conversation including with people you already know be they friends, relatives, work associates or casual acquaintances. There is an unending list of lead in questions to ask and you easily will pick-up on which of the topics they enjoy discussing:

"Where do you work?" – or – "What do you do?" This is good anywhere in the U.S. except in the South where the question is: "What church do you go to?"

"Do you have any children?"

"Do you have any grandchildren?"

"Have you been to a concert or good movie lately?"

"Where did you buy that beautiful dress?"

"Where are you planning to go on your vacation this year?"

"What is your favorite activity – other than your family of course?"

"Are you going to the ------------ festival this year?"

"What school did you attend?" If they name a college or university, then: "In what subject did you receive your degree?"

NUMBER 1 RULE during **_any_** conversation: **_NEVER_** after somebody has told you of something they did, saw, visited, or had anything whatsoever to do with in any manner whatsoever, never, never, ever, ever tell them that you did the same thing and make your story better than their story!!!! If you had a similar experience – tell them that you did something similar but explain to them how your experience came _nowhere near_ being even close to what their experience was. You just made a friend for life!

Even if your experience was spectacularly greater than the person with whom you are speaking – LIE!! Your experience in no way measures up – not even close. You will not go to Hell for that lie – I guarantee it! But, if you do, you can look me up and kick me around for all eternity since by having given you that advice, I'll have gotten there before you. Joke, LORD, joke – I'm not serious; I'm just trying to help folks here.

16.   Advertising. Now here's a trillion dollar a year industry that has built its foundation on "I, Me, My." (Amount spent per year is difficult to determine however adding up the various sources I could find pushed the amount to over a trillion dollars a year.) Next time you see an ad, in print or on TV, pay attention to the art and

science of what is being presented. How much meaningful information are they presenting to you? The ads will entertain you, glamorize the product, remove distractions from the product – you will seldom see competing products in the ad unlike in real life – and the tag line that is used over and over and over: "YOU _DESERVE_ ………."

It's amazing. Just by the very fact that you exist – regardless of your moral character, your income, your education, your job, your physical condition, your ability to use the product – just that fact that you were born and are alive at the time you see the ad, "YOU _DESERVE_ to have that product.

17.   Another of the sad I, Me, My results that we see are all the failed small businesses – especially restaurants.

A person has a great idea for a business. Of course it's a great idea – it's their idea. If it's my idea, it has to be great. If I really want it, so does everybody else. If I love my own cooking and my family loves my cooking (or so they say) and my friends love my cooking (or so they say also) then the whole world loves my cooking.

Back when I practiced law, I had many small business clients. Not being a financial advisor, I could not give them financial advice. However I would tell them grim stories of many failed businesses, I'd ask them if they had done any surveys or hired business advisors, spoken with their bank, spoken to representatives of the Small Business Administration, and all such warnings as I could.

From my undergraduate studies, I'd discuss certain portions of micro economics with them including opportunity costs. Finally they would either go someplace else because I made them uncomfortable and they felt I was discouraging them or they would go ahead with their idea and I'd make sure they didn't stub their toe on any legal rock in their path.

In addition to restaurant failures, I recall two ladies that had a fantastic idea that people would be lining up around the block at the craft shows to buy their product – this was before the electronic age of I-pads, PCs or any of the electronics we take for granted now – it was about a 5"x7" spiral note book into which you entered appointments, dates and phone numbers. I explained to them these could be purchased at just about any store that had school or office supplies. Oh, No! These had a place for recipes!!! I don't know how much money they put into having hundreds of these made. I doubt that they sold a dozen. But oh goodness – it was such a fantastic idea. I, Me, My.

18.   Politicians. What else needs to be said? Has there ever been a demographic that is more self-centered, more ego mania, more "I, Me, My" "It's all about me" than politicians? Politicians have made "I, Me, My" a science, an art and an industry.

They are totally shameless. Take any human tragedy – from acts of nature (floods, tornadoes, etc.) to human acts (mass shootings, kidnappings with loss of a child, etc.) and you can absolutely depend on politicians showing up with their phony concern to make sure that they get their face-time on TV and get their name out there.

If there isn't any real news to stick their nose into, they make up news. They will come up with some new cause, a new bill, making racial or sexual issue out of an occurrence no matter what the real facts are. At one time I did marketing (press releases, call press conferences, write speeches, write op-eds, etc. for politicians) and I've seen it all. Mea culpa, mea culpa – I'm sad to say that I was part of that process.

You'll see this in other demographics to lesser degrees. Many big business executives demonstrate such traits and in at least one case, the media (and the public) will make them a famous star. Of course we see it even in small business owners and even in some supervisors; to watch them and to listen to them you'd think they were the Emperor of the Universe – I believe we've all seen this at one time or another.

Then we have those in the entertainment industry – especially actors who begin to believe they are the parts they play. It's amazing that many in the general public accept these people as knowledgeable leadership figures. If you look into the background of many of these people you'll find high school drop-outs, people that couldn't even get into a community college, dysfunctional in personal relationships and many with criminal records and rampant alcohol and drug use. Yet much of the public is influenced by their opinion.

I once attended a performance by a well known entertainer in Portland, Oregon. She was on tour – city hopping, putting on her show. No doubt she could sing and dance and did that very well. At one point she took time to give her opinion on a purely local ballot measure of which she knew virtually nothing of the background or current details, but she sure told everybody there how they should vote.

During clean-up aftermath of Hurricane Katrina along the gulf coast, a very famous activist movie actor who jumps into the spotlight on every occasion he can was on TV ragging on the then current administration about the lousy job they were doing. Picture the scene: he's in a rowboat in an obviously flooded residential area. He's paddling the rowboat while talking (complaining) about what all isn't being done. All of a sudden, about 15 feet behind him a guy walks by from right to left wading in the water which isn't even up to his knees. OK, I know, mid-calf water is a lot to have in your street, but broadcasting from a rowboat you're paddling like you're in 30 feet of water? And remember – there's a national TV news network filming this!

Now there are many in the entertainment industries that do not impose themselves on the public in such a manner. Many do carry on very private lives and you never see anything of their political opinions in the news. (As an aside, I do not consider anything in the entertainment industry to be news.)

My favorite interview of an actor was one I saw where James Caan was interviewed. I don't recall his exact words so I'm paraphrasing but the gist is accurate. He said: "Acting is not something that an adult should do. That's what little kids do."

19. One more before we move on: "I want my gubumun check!" I'll break that word down: gub u mun. OK, even more: gov ern ment. Got it now? And, there's no racial, ethnic or other slur to "gubumun." That's just the way it so often sounds from the mouth of the "entitlement generation."

I was amazed, when in my mid 40s to find out that there were 3rd generation welfare people around – some I got to know because for one reason or another they became my clients - - not I did not represent them to pursue gubumun benefits. Now as I write this, some of those I met back then have children who followed them into the world of entitlement and at least one of them has young children also receiving their gubumun benefits – 5 generations and never paid taxes.

I recall in elementary school a teacher explaining to us that we should not look down on somebody who was out of a job and receiving unemployment compensation as they had paid into it for so long and they were now receiving what they needed until they could find a job. We understood that and I didn't think further about it for a very long time – until I began to become aware of abuses of the welfare system. And, lets not forget the expanding of the benefit system.

A pharmacist friend of mine who has lived in the area for all his life and seems to know almost everybody in this small town was telling me about how abusive many of the benefit recipients are when they pick-up their free meds. They are demanding immediate attention and are loud and impatient if not served immediately. One in particular he mentioned has never worked and her home, utilities, food, cell phone, prescriptions, her kids meals at school, their clothes, cell phones, etc., everything she has and all medical services are all paid for by the tax-payers – that's you an me.

If you ever talk to any of these people, they DESERVE to have everything because they exist. If anybody else has it (doesn't matter how hard the others work to obtain whatever) then they DESERVE it and will vote for whoever promises to deliver.

I have to thank a close friend for reminding me that I had left out the "entitlement" folks out of this section. That's really pretty bad that I've gotten so used to this being so much an everyday part of our society that I had originally overlooked it.

IN CONCLUSION consider this chapter as the foundation of all the other chapters. As you read through the chapters of this book, you'll begin to understand that everything is centered on the actor – the subject person. Everything is all about the individual to whom the event or issue pertains or to the individual upon whom the action occurs or who is taking the given action.

CHAPTER II

SEX
or
Survival of the Species

DID YOU EVER WONDER what would happen to any animal species wherein the members of that species would rather watch a beautiful sunset than copulate? The reason you can't find any such species is because its one of those "either – or" choices.

A species simply will not survive if there are – as a species as opposed to individually – any greater drive than reproducing. If sex isn't the number one drive of a species, it's going to die out. No babies, no species.

"Oh, but I love nice music, I love a good movie, I love reading a really good book." Sure; and some people love a cigarette – after sex.

Did you ever wonder why, in TV commercials they don't just have all average people of all ages in average clothes doing the acting. How about when you're in the store and walk by the area where they have books – did you ever notice that the "Romance" section is much larger than the section of books on art and philosophy, if they even have such a section. And what about the pictures on the front of those Romance books – it always shows a mousy couple conservatively dressed just standing or sitting properly side-by-side, right? Never!

How about the video games we see advertised – sex and violence. Some have more sex than violence and some have more violence than sex – it depends to which demographic they are trying to appeal. We see the same with TV programs and movies. There will be more about violence when we get to chapter VI; here we'll stay with sex, after all we want our species to survive.

So is this huge sex drive something real or did it just start? Well, let's see – humans have been making little humans for thousands or millions of years depending on which studies (or religions) you find convincing or with which you are comfortable. I think it's here to stay.

Let's take a look at our neighbors – no, don't go peeking in the bedroom window of the Jones' house next door. We'll look at the "animal kingdom" and (if you wish) you can make believe you're not an animal for now if you wish.

You've likely seen in nature segments on TV where male animals fight for mating rights with the females.

Commonly they will show you films of deer, elk and rams butting their antlers or horns against one another for dominance. That may give them a really bad headache but they may also prevail and have their choice of as many of the females as they can handle – or they just may go off horny until next season.

You can easily find other animals that go through serious physical competition in order to achieve dominance for mating. You'll find the same for such diverse creatures as sea turtles and giraffes.

While looking into what the members of various species find attractive in the opposite sex, I found that there is a real difference in what each gender finds attractive in the other. These differences in sexual attraction are based on what each sex finds not necessary in the other. An obvious example is the antlers on a male deer. Over a great deal of time this causes a significant difference in appearance between the genders. This phenomenon is referred to as "sexual dimorphism" and makes for interesting reading – much too academic for our purposes here.

For some animals, procreation is a lot more serious than ending up with a headache or horny. There are a number of marsupials that give their all – they die after mating. There are so many species of insects and spiders where this occurs – it is quite common. A few instances of dying for sex would include some bees, black widows and the mantis. Some manners of their dying are quite interesting. You can search that out on your own if interested – such things as bursting testicles and the female killing and eating the male.

Now that we've considered our animal friends, let's take a look at us humans. Recall now, that humans have this great intellect – IQs that leave the animals' way, way in the back of the class. We have all that nice big cerebral cortex that allows us to really think about our actions – to consider consequences, an imagination, self control and not to just act on our urges.

So let's consider just what we do with all that brain power:

Just how strong is this sex drive thing with humans? You likely have heard (especially you guys) somebody say something like: "Man what I wouldn't give to get that one in the sack." If you've never seen it in person, you certainly have seen it in movies where some guys get into a fight over a woman – in the movies occasionally it leads to death.

You likely have also seen what I call the "Saturday Night Posture." This is a "civilized" form of competition. It seems that over my lifetime that the Saturday Night Posture has been slowly expanding until now we see much of it as daily routine among some people. This is where the ladies make themselves up to trigger every possible arousal that will set a guy off in pursuit.

There have been studies that discuss the ratio of a woman's waist size to hip size. Other studies have determined how a woman appears when ovulating or is ready and wanting sexual contact. Others have demonstrated what attracts men – usually those things that indicate a woman would be a good one for procreation which includes the waist-hips ratio and large breasts.

Guys will also try to do their Saturday Night Posturing. They try to make themselves appear as masculine as possible. To have the appearance of the good hunter that can provide and protect. Even those who appear to have taken very little time and look a bit disheveled spent a great deal of time getting just "that look" – heck they probably have a pedicure.

The ladies in putting on their Saturday Night Posture, use make up and wardrobe to accentuate the ready for sex look. The eye make-up: when ready, a lady's eyes open wide and pupils dilate - the eye make-up draws attention to the eyes. The rouge or other facial make-up mimics the facial blush when the blood rushes toward the surface of her face when she's ready. The red lipstick does the same as the other facial make-up.

Her wardrobe, cinches in the waist, lifts and accentuates the breasts and often shows her cleavage – sometimes a very large amount of cleavage. The guys' pants come up to the waist (except for punk gang-bangers – most of whom have no clue where that trend started or they wouldn't do it) whereas the ladies come up to only mid-hip to accentuate that hip to waist ratio.

For the guys it's very easy to understand the effort they put in as the ladies can and are very selective. There are more men out on the hunt on any given Saturday Night than there are ladies. The guys have to do all they can to attract a lady. On the other hand all a lady has to do is show up.

Don't think for an instant that just because women do all this stuff to arouse guys that don't need any arousing and just because they may flaunt their sexuality that I'm making any sort of excuse for the bad conduct of some men. As far as I'm concerned, any guy that physically and/or sexually abuses a woman should be made physically unable to ever have sex again for the rest of his life – and it should be done in the most painful way possible. That's before they go to prison for a minimum of 40 years.

* * * * * * *

Just a quick look at the darker side: We have all either read about and/or seen reports on TV, more times than we can count of rape. Rarely is it a woman raping a man – pretty hard for a man to have an erection while threatened or beaten. About the only reports of women involved in rape are the cases of statutory rape where a school teacher has sexual relations with one of her male students.

Another common category of rape are homosexual rapes, most of which occur in prisons and occur in both male and female prisons. I have represented a prisoner who was a rape victim and the information he provided me confirmed what I had already heard of from other sources and information which I had read. While not uncommon, it is not something that we find often reported.

There is also "the world's oldest profession" – prostitution. There is both male and female prostitution. Prostitution however is not the only sex for money industry. There is a thriving pornography industry. There are "Adult" stores in most major cities where you can buy pornographic DVDs of most any persuasion you wish.

Not all of the pornography industry (including child pornography) reports earnings, but most reports indicate that in the U.S. its gross annual income is in the range of $20 billion a year and growing. World wide it is estimated that the industry is in the range of $60 billion a year.

Even darker is the sex slave industry. There are about 500,000 of these victims a year with an age range of 8 years to 23 years. World wide it's the third biggest criminal enterprise – right after drugs and guns. The annual income is estimated at $32 billion a year. The U.S. isn't immune. It is estimated that that within the U.S. there are 15,000 victims annually – not all brought in from outside the country.

These statistics come from multiple sources and are roughly the average of the reported amounts. Some of the sources I consider fairly reliable such as charities with the mission of helping the victims and from the U.S. State Department. Other sources I consider somewhat less reliable. However with checking so many different sources, it appears that all the numbers are fairly consistent which causes me to think that all are reporting fairly accurate numbers. You can do your own further research but its pretty disgusting stuff.

This foregoing was not presented to shock, but rather to demonstrate how deeply ingrained and strong is the absolute "need" for sex dwells within humans.

However, one last item on the dark side of the irresistible compulsive need for sex at any cost: Necrophilia. Yep, it's what it sounds like. One year when I was the officer in charge of Shore Patrol (US Navy equivalent of Military Police) at a particular celebratory port of call, a sailor was arrested for mutilating a corpse.

This port had the reputation for the easiest place to get laid of any place you could visit as a sailor. I guess this sailor couldn't even score there. He got caught for braking into a funeral home and having sex with one of their customers.

With that, I have to relay a not true story of humor. We humans can seem to find humor in most any subject somehow:

Some time ago, in Paris, France, a man was on trial for having had sex with a corpse. The very angry magistrate said to the man: "You are despicable! Don't you understand that as a Frenchman you not only have your own reputation to think of in the matters of sex, but of our entire country? We French have a world reputation as to our loving! How could you possibly have sex with a dead woman?

The accused responded: "Your Excellency, I didn't know she was dead. I thought she was English."

****

Let's now turn to a bit of history about how screwed up (no pun intended) we are when it comes to sex. How we humans can really mess up our own lives and the lives of others to the point of destroying entire countries.

How far back in history would you like to go to start our observations of sex – or – propagating the species? Shall we start with the Book of Genesis in the Bible? In Genesis chapter 34 we have Shechem who saw, took and lay with Dinah. This would have been around 1900 BCE.

We can move a bit north and see another bit of irresistible propagation. Remember the phrase: The face that launched 1,000 ships? Yep, around 1200 BCE we've got Helen of Sparta – later Helen of Troy – with Paris of Troy and Menelaus. This was good for a war of about 10 years (the Trojan War) and how many lives?

We can jump back to the Bible with one of the heroes of the old Testament: David – as in David and Goliath – who, when he was walking around on the roof of his palace one night, saw a beautiful woman bathing below on another roof top. The woman was Bathsheba who happened to be the wife of one of David's army's heroes – Uriah. Well, David just had to have her so he had her brought to him – kings could do that back then. Check 2 Samuel, chapter 11.

David later had one of his Generals, Joab, put Uriah in the most dangerous place in the front lines during battle and abandon him. Poor old Uriah. David had his fling with Bathsheba around 1,000 BCE.

Let's take a big leap forward in time staying with only the most popularly known sexcapades. From around 35 BCE to 30 BCE we had Anthony and Cleopatra getting together to Julius Caesar's chagrin. Well that didn't go well for them. Long battle, Anthony and Cleopatra both commit suicide. The good news was that was the end of the civil wars for Rome and the Roman Empire was consolidated. Again, lots of people died horrid deaths.

We can take another big jump forward – up to the early 1500s CE. Good old King Henry VIII. There have been movies, books and songs made about this guy's escapades. He even ended the domination of the Catholic Church in England and had a new church started over his need to propagate. The Catholic Church would not allow him to divorce. That simply does not work for a guy who ended up having had six wives during his lifetime: one died supposedly of natural causes, two had their heads cut off, two of them he divorced and one out lasted him.

During this time – Shechem to Henry VIII – the estimated population of the earth increased from about 25 million to 500 million. The basic need to propagate – sex – was doing pretty good considering the lack of medical science, poor diet, poor shelter and war. That was a period of about 3,400 years. Since then, in the last about 600 years we've managed to grow from ½ billion to 7 billion. What's really impressive is that this phenomenal growth is with major wars, genocide and birth control. I think we've just about got that propagation thing down really good.

Moving to more modern examples of the sex drive and its damage to relationships is found both in fiction – which is meant to reflect real life – and to the real world. Looking in the historical order in which they occurred, we can first consider the popular book and movie "Gone With the Wind." We have Rhett Butler, Scarlett O'hara and Ashley Wilkes. Of course with Scarlett, we may have more of a pentagon than a triangle – but basically a love triangle.

Another book and movie would be the "Titanic." No, sex did not sink the Titanic, but there is as a main theme, a typical love triangle in the movie. The female lead falls for the more masculine, irresponsible young man sailing in the lowest class accommodations and leaving her very rich fiancé. It was all about which one is going to be really fun and exciting (another word for sex?) for her.

Keeping with the movies, we have Rick Blaine, Ilsa Lund and Victor Lazlo as the love triangle. This triangle had pretty much the same outcome as Titanic. The exciting guy gets left. If you didn't recognize the names, those are the main characters in "Casablanca."

Before leaving the world of sex and fiction, I can't help but to throw in Betty, Archie and Veronica of comic book fame. I just had to mention them. Even there in innocent comics we find the topic just under the surface.

****

Now we'll turn to some real life famous examples of the strength of the sex drive. Those who prefer to call those books "romance novels" instead of "smut" can call the following "true love" if it makes you more comfortable. Some of the following were less destructive than others, but in all cases there were either injury to an individual, too many and even to a historic change for a country.

In England in 1936 King Edward VIII had fallen in love with an American divorcee, Wallis Simpson, and he abdicated his thrown to marry her. There was a movie made where his character filled a small part, his brother was the main character, George VI – "Kings Speech."

During the filming of "Cleopatra," Elizabeth Taylor (Cleopatra) and her co-star Richard Burton (Mark Antony) really got into their characters. Taylor was married to Eddie Fisher at the time. At least all Eddie got was divorced – he didn't suffer Uriah's fate.

One of the most famous and recent of these love triangles was that of Prince Charles, Princess Diana and Camilla Parker Bowles. Well at least he didn't have Princess Diana's head cut off. He did cast a bit of a cloud on the Royal Family. Sometimes I wonder if the Queen may have retired had Charles not divorced Diana. Poor Diana, what a short, amazing life she had.

****

Then we have those who have made it to very high positions in life and that darned old irresistible sex drive stuff just destroyed them (with one notable exception) – usually taking many who loved them down with them. On one rare occasion, it didn't seem to matter, but then politics and politicians are almost a species of their own and hard to figure.

We'll start with the exception. Usually a sex scandal will destroy a powerful elected public official. I'm sure you've already guessed who the exception was. That's right, President Bill Clinton. Monica Lewinsky first showed up at the White House in 1995 and later obtained a full time position at that most prestigious location. Bill's and Monica's sexual escapades pretty much dominated the news in 1998 when their sexual activities became a topic of everyday conversation.

Bill lied, lied, lied. He even got caught lying under oath. There was absolutely no doubt about it that he committed a criminal act – lying under oath. He was impeached. However, this is politics at its _finest_. He was not found guilty. It mattered not that there could be no doubt whatsoever that he lied under oath.

You may even remember the famous very weak non-answer he gave to a question where he stated something to the effect of "It depends on what the meaning of "is" is."

That he was receiving oral sex from Monica right there in the White House, during working hours when he has the solemn obligation to assure the welfare of the U.S. and all its citizens and the obligations of the U.S. around the world, Bill, a married man with a minor daughter, is getting a blow job in his office.

At least when President Richard Nixon was caught lying – not under oath – and spying on the Democrats (gee nothing like that goes on now) he had the decency to resign.

Bill, on the other hand, after getting caught in a sex scandal, lying under oath and denying the most obvious of sexual inappropriate conduct stayed in office and remains an American political icon.

I can't decide if Bill's status says as much about forgiveness as it does about our society's gross loss of a moral compass. I suppose it could also say something about which side of the aisle you sit on. Then again, as you'll see immediately below, both sides of the aisle have been hammered for their aggressive and sometimes odd obsessive sexual conduct.

Moving along our timeline, we come to U.S. Senator John Edwards. In the early 2000s he was a rising political star. He made a run for the U.S. presidency in 2004 and in 2008. In the general election of 2004 he was the candidate for Vice President, on the ticket with John Kerry running for President. Many, including a close relative of mine, were very much enamored by John. He had that polished handsome appearance and that soft southern voice.

He was especially appealing to his girlfriend by whom he had a child – all of which he kept hidden for a long time. By the way, this was all while his wife, Elizabeth, was terminally ill with cancer. He often used Elizabeth as a prop during his campaign. She has since passed away. John's not running for anything anymore.

Moving right along with the sex – pardon me; procreation – driven people, we move to U.S. Senator Larry Craig. He was finally arrested for his activities in trying to find a sex partner in the men's restroom in a Minnesota airport. When he was questioned about trying to play footsie with the man sitting in the next stall, he said that was not the case. Larry said he just has a very wide stance. I don't think the average person is capable of coming up with these weird excuses; it must be something down deep in politicians' DNA. "Wide stance." "It depends on what "is" is."

Next on the timetable we have U.S. Representative Anthony Weiner. Could the guy have had a more appropriate name or what? I'd never heard of the term "sexting" until good old Weiner became a regular news item in 2011. Here's this U.S. Congressman, got it made, powerful position, famous, really good salary, benefits and very little work, a staff of people doing all of his bidding, rubbing shoulders with the rich, famous and powerful.

So what's sex obsessed Weiner start doing, he's taking naked (or partially naked) pictures of himself in front of a mirror with the camera on his cell phone or I-phone or whatever and putting it out there – wherever "out there" is with all this electronic stuff; I suppose only the NSA really knows. He goes through all the silly denials then, as most gets to the mea culpa stuff and finally resigns.

Here's what should be amazing about the Weiner incident, but the American voters no longer shock or even surprise me. He recently ran for mayor of New York City. He came in 5th out of 9 candidates in that primary. However, it's still a bit difficult to imagine how this guy could have found 31,874 people that voted for him. That's a lot of very strange people.

We'll wrap up with one of the most recent of these guys whose brains just can't overcome that basic compulsive need to keep the species going: Mayor Bob Filner of San Diego, California. How do these guys get elected in the first place? There has to have been some indication of what kind of person they were somewhere along the line – I don't believe these behaviors just start out of the blue. But then again, we've all seen on TV where some reporter manages to find a neighbor of the just arrested axe-murderer who says "Oh, he was a nice quiet guy and such a good neighbor."

What did Bob do? He chased nearly every female he came into contact with in his position as Mayor. The last count I heard was that there were 19 formal complaints against him. After the usual denials and lame excuses, he pleads guilty and was sentenced to house arrest for a short period and three years probation.

There used to be a saying about the difference between Democrat and Republican scandals. Republicans got caught getting into somebody's pocket book and

Democrats got caught getting into somebody's pants. I find no political party affiliation to be any indicator whatsoever. Those unable to control their sexual urges are found everywhere and anywhere at all times. The above mentioned men of position and power fell regardless of what side of the aisle they were on:

Bill Clinton	Democrat
John Edwards	Democrat
Larry Craig	Republican
Anthony Weiner	Democrat
Bob Filner	Democrat

While the Democrats seem to have a bit more of a numerical edge, I'll chalk that up to Republicans, in being a bit more conservative; take a little more care not to get caught.

* * * * * * *

For the loving, caring, touchy-feely, politically correct, I must touch on the subject of how procreation, the survival of the species, and the care and protection of our children are at the forefront of our instincts. This issue was brought up to me by having it pointed out that I should see what would happen to me if I were to "get between a momma bear and her cubs." I think we've all heard this phrase used multiple times as *the* example for this issue. I don't know how many times I've heard about the "momma bear and her cubs."

We do often see the grieving parent on TV news asking for help to find their lost child, or for the safe return of their child who was taken by either an unknown person or by the non-custodial parent. This makes for good TV ratings so we see it played over and over – TV producers using horrid human tragedy for ratings.

On nature programs we see more than the "momma bear." We see birds diving through the air at other birds – often much larger than they – to protect their eggs or young in their nests. The penguins in sub freezing weather standing for days to keep their eggs warm. We see whales swimming with their young protecting and caring for them.

In the movies we often see scenes of parents protecting their children from the invaders – be they human, animals or aliens. It is so deep within us that the act comes without conscious thought – more as a reflex than an instinct. It's hard to think of a parent – the average, normal parent – that would not give their life for their child.

So it is argued that it's not just about sex. Well, they're right – to a degree. However with humans, contraception is a huge industry. The last figure I saw is that a bit over $17 billion is spent on contraception per year. Sounds like a great deal of money being spent for the purpose of having sex in a manner specifically designed not to propagate the species. And contraception devices are not new. I recall reading that one of King Henry VIII wives used a common contraception device of the time – she inserted a small pebble into her vagina to keep from getting pregnant. I don't recall which wife that was – it may have cost her, her head.

If I didn't believe it necessary for our discussion, I would not even mention the topic of the approximate one million legal abortions performed annually in the U.S. alone. Regardless of one's position on the topic, that sure isn't sex for propagation of the species.

I also mentioned in the Introduction the mentally deranged; which, in the animal kingdom, seems to be limited to the human species. Too frequently we hear of the boyfriend who has shaken his girlfriend's baby to death or the young woman who discards her newborn into a dumpster. I'll make no further mention of the mentally deranged in the following chapters as they are an anomaly even though they are among us.

Of course, if one were to believe in reincarnation, perhaps they will receive their just desserts: Maybe these evil people comeback as spiders. Perhaps as a male spider who is killed by the female after sex or who otherwise dies after sex. Better yet as the female spider. When the eggs hatch and those zillion little bitty spiders need nourishment right away – their first meal is their mother.

I suppose we just can't leave this topic without mentioning homosexuality – sex between members of the same gender. That such sexual relations have nothing to do with propagation of the species falls into that "well duh" category. So, it's obviously just plain old sex for the sake of satisfying the irresistible need for sex.

But is homosexuality common throughout the animal kingdom? I'm not going to take the time to do a lot of research on the topic, but I have seen it practiced by canines. Beyond what I've seen, my lack of interest in the topic is immense.

Some seem to think that sex among persons of the same gender is something new. While I'm aware from my own reading of it being extremely common and considered normal in ancient Greece, I have found little on this topic in history texts. There also are several references in the Bible to homosexual activity in times millennia ago. I'll take it from such references that obvious non-propagation sex has been around a very long time.

CHAPTER III

NEVER DO IT THE HARD WAY

LION CHASES THE ZEBRA; did you ever wonder why the lion doesn't go after the really fast big zebra at the front? Why does the lion always go after the smaller one at the rear? The one in front is always bigger. Does the lion just like the more tender meat of the younger zebra? No! The lion's just lazy. Saying its lazy doesn't mean that it isn't really strong and fast, it's just going to take the easiest route to getting a good meal.

Regardless where you've seen it – TV or movies, National Geographic, other documentaries or dramas – we've all seen the fast, strong predator going after its prey. The predator always, always, goes for the one that is slow or lame – the easiest one they can catch and kill for dinner.

Most domestic pets are predators – dogs and cats. Do they refuse to eat that really great tasty stuff that their owners put in their bowls and instead go hunt, chase and kill their dinner? Regardless of in the wild or domestic, the animals take the easy way to a meal.

Even those animals which are not predators take the easy way. I've never seen a herd of cattle walk to the far end of the field or to the highest hill in the field to graze if the farmer has placed bales of hay in convenient locations for them. How about all those nice people who put out bird feeders or spread birdseed around their yards? Do the birds instead of feeding on these easy meals instead choose to search for other sources?

Animals take the easy way – even to their detriment at times. Consider hunting season and fishing season. Hunters – where it's legal (and sometimes even if it's not) will place feed in certain areas which will attract the animal they are hunting. That animal, taking the easy way to a meal, ends up a meal. Fisherman do the same – they offer the fish an easy meal and the fish too become a meal.

You can see the natural instinct of animals to do it the easy way in migration. There are a surprising number of animals which migrate: bats, geese, crabs, whales, salmon, wildebeests, dragonflies and caribou just to name a few. As far as I've been able to determine, none of them take significant side trips to go sightseeing – they just take the most efficient route to get to where they're going. OK sometimes whales have beached themselves and other odd occurrences show up in the news, but over all they do it the easy way.

All of these "lazy" activities are for a very good purpose among animals in the wild. They are preserving their resources. Food supplies are limited and take a great deal of work – burning up more reserves – to acquire. They live efficiently. You do not see fat animals in the wild; except those who are about to hibernate such as bears, skinks, bats, frogs, snakes and some insects will gain extra weight (reserves) just prior to hibernation.

Animals' sleep patterns also reflect their instinctive conduct to maintain reserves. Really big animals sleep very little because they have to spend a great deal of time eating to survive. Elephants only sleep about 3 hours a day while some bats sleep more than 18 hours a day to store their reserve for their eating frenzy during the short time each day that flying insects are available to them.

Now with all our brain power – which we've previously mentioned – how do we handle this very natural "never do it the hard way" tendency or instinct? Surely we've come up with really magnificent concepts and methods of not unnecessarily depleting our reserves. What comes to mind right away? Ah, the TV remote!

After some delay, I get back to writing. This chapter has been difficult to start writing – I just couldn't come up with the energy to get off my lazy backsides to get to writing.

When it comes to "Never do it the hard way" we virtually all have a lot in common. Just as we've seen in our above discussion with the animals why spend extra energy to accomplish a task when we can do it a simpler and easier way? After all, extra work just burns up additional resources and we must look out for our survival – we never know when we'll have another meal.

I recall reading a really great novel by Ken Follett titled "Pillars of the Earth." The book was set in roughly the 1200s. Distances were measureD in how many days it would take to walk to the destination. When there was food available, you ate all you could because you truly did not know when you would eat again.

Not in Follett's book, but we take so many things for granted and don't even think about all that we have that makes life easy. Up until the 1800s only the wealthy and elite could afford candles or lamps of any sort – when the sun went down you were in complete darkness until sunrise. For much of our not too remote human history, less than 5% of the people could read.

With our intellect, we have been able to become so efficient that we have made life extremely easy. We have to do very little to survive. We have made industry and entertainment out of using our natural physical energies. We pay to go to the gym to exercise – of course we drive to the gym. And, if you just take time to look around, you can see that not all that many people go to the gym. It seems that weekly we have an item in the news about obesity.

****

Let's take a look at our lazy habits and all that we have that encourages such laziness:

1.   When you drive into the parking lot at the store, do you park far away from the entrance or close? If you have a really nice vehicle and you are very fussy about it, then you may park a ways away so that careless (or jealous) people don't put dents in the sides when they open their doors.

However, we've all seen people that will drive around and around near the entrance waiting for an opening as near the door as possible. Burn up $3.00 worth of gas to keep from walking a few feet. And of course we see a number of handicap parkers who when they get out of their car and go into the store, the only thing obviously wrong with them is that they're too lazy to walk.

While we're talking about stores, what did all those people do before they had those motorized carts in all the big stores? They seem just fine getting to the cart, cruising around the store then getting back in their car.

Another one at the store parking lot: Just about all the grocery store lots have racks where you can safely place your cart to keep it out of the way of those trying to park or leave the lot. Have you ever been in one of those lots where some people left the carts wherever they wanted and didn't bother walking a few feet to place the cart in the rack?

2.   The store – any store – or the post office or whatever is about ¼ to ½ mile from home. How many people will walk short distances instead of driving? Not too many. When we first moved to the small town we now live in, after about a couple of months, I heard that many people referred to me as "Oh that older guy that walks around town."

3.   Another thriving industry is car washes. Now there's something that is really unpleasant labor. Who would ever want to wash their car in their own drive way or in front of their house on a nice sunny day? That's way too labor intensive! We'll just spend several dollars on gas, wear and tear on our car and pay at the car wash to have somebody else – or some machine – wash it for us. After all, we wouldn't want to take even a chance on working up a sweat or having our heart rate increase a few ticks.

4.   We could talk about power tools, but those can be a lot of work and the efficiency they give to our society, makes most of them a plus overall. Yet, they do reduce the amount of labor one puts into any project.

5.   Here are a couple of little ones that when you think about them as lazy items, are kind of funny: Velcro straps instead of shoe laces and one-button speed dialing.

Mentioning speed dialing, how about all those email acronyms? There's those that are most common and used even by some who are not too awfully lazy (BTW), but some just fly in your face:

AML	All my love.
DFWLY	Don't forget who loves you.
ILU	I love you.
LOML	Love of my life.
LUMU	Love you, miss you.
YLH	Your loving husband.
YLW	Your loving wife.

Now tell me, is that true love or what? They can't even bother to take the time to write out the message! They just punch in letters! Just what message are they sending? Kind of like, "I'd make love to you, but that's too much work – I'll just do it myself."

6.   Domestic help. What can I say? Having been raised in a home where domestic help (indoors or outside) was something you only saw in the movies – pure fantasy, nobody had any kind of domestic help. Well, there were perhaps three or four households in the neighborhood that would have a kid mow their lawn for a dollar.

When I say we saw such things in the movies, I mean the three or four times I went to the movies each year. Going to the movies was a special treat back then and an all afternoon event. Always a double feature – that's two full length movies – plus a news reel, plus a cartoon and also previews of coming movies. These outings would cost me a quarter – 20 cents to get into the movie and 5 cents for candy!

Now it seems that most folks have people that either come to clean their house or work in their yard or both. There are franchises that people purchase to take advantage of national or regional advertising although many just work on their own out of their homes. Domestic help is so widespread that there are many specialties such as carpet cleaning and window washing.

7.   Government hand-outs. There's a topic that will raise the volume in any room any where any time with any demographic mix. I can hear it now – on one side those who shout about paying too much in taxes and how those who receive the hand-outs are just lazy. On the other side you have those who are just as committed to the idea that the government doesn't do enough for those in need.

The volume continues to rise. "I've paid taxes every year and worked everyday for a hundred years and those lazy good for nothings won't get off their backsides and get a job!" To which you hear something like: "I never got to get no education. I had to take care of all my children. I lived in a poor area where there were no jobs. My daddy could never find work. The government didn't give me enough money to get all the stuff I needed – I didn't even have a new pair of Nikes or an iPhone until I was 10 years old!"

Now we're really getting emotional and nobody is going to hear anything the other side says; and for good reason – neither side is saying anything rational.

"Government hand-outs." A loaded term and I used it on purpose. I could have said something to the effect of "government benefits" or "government incentives" or "public assistance" or "workers compensation" or "unemployment compensation" or "Social Security benefits" or "government pension payments" – but – all of these come from some government entity (some government retirement programs place their money into private investment funds) but they are all primarily paid by the tax payers and received primarily by the non-workers, non-tax payers.

Is there anybody out there that would not like to receive something for nothing? That demographic has to be in the high 90s as to percent range. So here we are back to politicians. What politician was ever elected by promising everybody that if elected government payments were going to be severely cut? What politician ever got elected that promised everybody that the rules to qualify for disability, unemployment compensation and worker's compensation were going to be severely tightened? What politician ever got elected promising that college benefits would have to be earned by working for a period of years then going to college? What politician was ever elected by telling his/her constituency that they were irresponsible parents who allow their kids to not go to school, drink, use illicit drugs, steal and make babies in their early teens?

Since everybody 18 or older who is not a felon (maybe) can vote, what kind of politician are they going to vote for? For the one who promises to hold them accountable? For the one who promises more government hand-outs?

While it's easy to blame the politician, remember – they would not be in power if they had not been voted into their position by a majority of those who bothered to vote.

* * * * * * *

Let's jump into the mentally lazy for just a little while and for a change of pace – now that I got your blood pressure up regardless of your political view point.

Some obvious examples of mentally lazy would include:

1.   Kids can no longer multiply or divide – they have at least calculators if not computers to do all that sort of work. Who needs any basic math skills?

2.   While I type this book, my computer corrects my spelling and my grammar. If you find grammatical errors – that's where I argued with the computer and I won.

3.   Compared to other "developed" countries, our kids score very low in tests. I lay much of that on politicians who get into how schools should be run and push to dumb-down testing. "Politicians" also include school board members, but I'm also referring to those at

the state and national level who use schools and students to their own purposes.

An example of the politics in schools is when there is a measure for school funding. The supporters always roll out the kids – especially little kids in front of the camera on their ads. Sometime check after the levy has been passed to see just how much of that money gets to the class room in the shape of something that will improve the kids' education.

The formation of the U.S. Department of Education has done little – perhaps moved us backward. We had the "No Child Left Behind" federal legislation and program. Why is it that when we know the government fails at every task it takes on – except perhaps war; and there's an argument there – we keep electing politicians that want to give us more government and keep throwing good money after bad.

At best, U.S. students have been stagnant while other countries are advancing. In recent comparative scores, the rankings of a few of the countries are as follows:

Country Science	Math	Reading
Shanghai	620	570
580		
Singapore		
Japan	(All these	
Korea	in fairly	

Netherlands		evenly spaced
Switzerland		descending order)
Poland		
Canada		
U.S.	480	490

485

I don't believe that U.S. kids have some sort of innate inability to learn just because they are raised on this particular piece of ground on the Earth. The major problem that I see is the continuous deterioration of the social standards in the U.S. which includes the family, entertainment and government – all combining to create generations of lazy and lazier. However, each one _DESERVES_ to have all those wonderful toys and benefits.

Of course we don't really know just how bad the U.S. score is since we have such a high drop-out rate. If we could round up all of the drop-outs and have them tested also, we'd probably find ourselves numerically on the list about where we'd be if listed in alphabetical order.

4.   Other signs of mental laziness:

Messy and filthy homes; everything just lies where it lands.

Cars; ever see a car that looks like a messy filthy house?

Audio books; it takes too much effort to actually read.

Soaps and Sit-coms; you can just watch life, why live it?

5.   In some cases, doctors will put a name on it, treat it, and prescribe drugs for it. Insurance companies will collect from you (and in some cases and/or from the government) and pay for the treatment and the drugs. There are some people with legitimate mental issues but some are despondent out of convenience and some are addicted to their prescriptions.

6.   One sort of mental laziness that has been given a name is a very frustrating one. Think what you will as to its legitimacy. "Passive – Aggressive." I've seen this one several times and in at least one case – maybe two – I've seen it breakup a marriage. The passive-aggressive person will agree with whatever is asked: "Don't do that." "OK" and then they continue with whatever the behavior was. "Do that." "OK" and then they don't do it. Never argue, never violent and always agree – then they just keep on doing everything their own way. What a lazy way to drive somebody crazy.

Over the last couple of centuries we've seen a country created on the highest of ideals with absolute belief in the sanctity of the individual and which demanded complete personal responsibility reach to the undisputed peak of world status. People from all over the world risk everything to move here. Through our slovenly laziness as a people we now see the U.S. crumbling and deteriorating.

CHAPTER IV

EAT WHEN IT'S AVAILABLE

EVEN EACH OTHER? Well, for some in the animal kingdom, yes. But we won't quite get into the particular eating habits of the animal kingdom just yet. Some of those habits we won't discuss here – but for those of you with really weird ideas of what's interesting, you can do your own research. It gets to be pretty unusual and not exactly dinner conversation for us who consider ourselves normal.

First, let's talk about types of diets by various animals. While plants "eat" also – some more like animals than you'd think – we'll stick to the animal world. Here are the types of animals we have by type of diet:

HERBIVORE: Herbivore, as with the rest of the "vore" categories, the root of the last part of the word comes from the Latin *vorare,* meaning "to devour." In the case of herbivore, we have those animals which eat <u>only</u> plant materials such as leaves, grass and bark. These animals have teeth made for grinding and their digestive systems are also adapted to such a diet. Among the common herbivores are deer, horses and cattle.

Herbivores are at the <u>bottom</u> of the food chain.

CARNIVORE: Here we have those that eat <u>only</u> flesh. This category is divided into two groups; the first are the predators – those who will hunt and chase down their prey, kill it and eat it. This kind of reminds me of *Acts 10:13* "... *"Rise, Peter; kill and eat."*" Maybe not – see the next category.

The second group in the Carnivore category is the scavengers – they only eat the flesh of those who have already been killed or otherwise died. However, if a predator is hungry – and they nearly always are – they are not above passing up a free meal.

Carnivores have sharp teeth, claws and eyes that face front that give them depth perception for chasing down prey – meals. There's an exception to the eyes facing forward: crocodiles. Crocodiles' eyes are on the sides, but then they don't chase down their prey, they ambush them.

Common examples of Carnivores are lions (which eat 15 pounds of flesh a day), tigers, wolves and panthers – all of these eat only flesh.

OMNIVORES: My favorite! They'll eat anything that won't eat them back – and they'll even eat those if they get to take the first bite. They aren't the least bit fussy. If they're hungry, they're going to eat their fill of anything available.

"Omni" means "everything/all" from its Latin root. You already saw above that the "vore" part means "to devour," so these Omnivores are those that devour everything and all things. You want to argue about the "devour everything and all things" part? Check the below comments when we get to the Tiger Shark.

These animals have a combination of sharp and grinding teeth and digestive systems that will accommodate anything (most anything – again see the Tiger Shark below) going through their system.

Common examples of Omnivores include: bears, orangutans, hedgehogs, skunks, pigs, rats and humans.

* * * * * * *

We'll take a quick look at some of the more interesting eating habits of our animal friends:

First and foremost for our purposes, they eat whenever it's available. Not when they're completely full of course – not necessarily so. Most, yes, will stop eating when they can no longer get another bite into their system. Remember that all these very close family members of ours have no idea when they will get a chance to eat again – and – historically it wasn't that long ago for us humans either. Read Ken Follett's *Pillars of the Earth*.

When you can't run down to McDonald's or the local grocery store when you're hungry – most wolves, bears, and skunks don't have that opportunity – you eat when it's available and eat your fill because you don't know when you will eat again. Hard to imagine, but think about it for a while.

Now we can finally get to the Tiger Shark! Their eating habits start very young. Before they are born, while inside the mother, they are eating each other! You can look that one up yourself. Inside of Tiger Sharks that have been caught, has been found things as diverse as license plates and shoes. Now that there's an Omnivore to be proud of! The Tiger Shark should be placed on a pedestal at the Omnivore Museum – if there was such a thing.

Vultures – yuk; even though they serve a really necessary function in the ecosystem. They devour 20% of their body weight at one sitting. Yum!

Tasmanian Devil: Yep, there really is a Tasmanian Devil. This creature makes the just named vulture look like a piker. This guy (or gal) will eat up to 40% of its body weight in 30 minutes.

Argentine Widemouth Frog: What can you say about this one? This one may be the most absurd of the bunch – maybe not, but if not first, it's a very close second. It will gorge itself until it actually rips its stomach and dies.

Blue Whale: For sheer volume, you simply cannot beat the Blue Whale – not now, not the dinosaurs. Krill are a non-vertebrae sea creature. Blue Whales eat Krill. Blue Whales eat <u>40 million Krill a day</u> – except during breeding season. Granted the Blue Whale is the largest animal that has ever lived on this rock we call Earth, and, Krill are very small, but – 40 million a day!!! WOW seems so inadequate an exclamation.

Caterpillar: Three cheers for the little guy. Regardless of size, we have to acknowledge a champion by performance compared to what they are. The absolute champion is the Caterpillar. It's a very good thing for all of us that it is such a very small creature. The Caterpillar eats 1,000 times its weight in two months.

So, if the Caterpillar was the size of a Blue Whale, it would eat approximately 380,000,000 pounds of food in two months. I wonder why there's never been a horror movie about a giant Caterpillar.

Just a quick touch on what we humans would consider extreme eating habits. To name a few animals in this last category, consider Tiger Sharks (again), Polar Bears, Hamsters, Tiger Salamanders (something about "Tiger"?) and many of the rodent family. <u>These all eat their young.</u> But then if you read Dr. Charles Krauthammer's essay *On the Ethics of Embryonic Research,* The New Republic, April 29, 2002, as presented in his book *Things That Matter,* Crown Forum, 2013 – are we humans far behind? – figuratively speaking of course.

* * * * * * *

Finally, we can move on to us humans. We just can't match up to our animal friends. The average – "average" not the huge eaters, but just the average – U.S. citizen eats about 1,700 pounds a year. 1,700 pounds of food a year amounts to about 6 McDonald's Quarter Pounders for each of breakfast, lunch and dinner – wow, 18 Quarter Pounders a day.

Of course, U.S. citizens consume more calories per person that the citizens of any other country on the planet. Here's a list of just a few countries and the calorie intake per person:

USA	3770
Italy	3660
UK	3440
Russia	3270
Iran	3040
China	2970
Jamaica	2850
Panama	2450
Switzerland	2310
Pakistan	2250
Palestine	2130
Haiti	1850

Not surprising, the U.S. also has the highest disposable income per person. Haiti's yearly personal income is $400.

Not being scientific, but just using a bit of common sense here. If you have the highest income and an abundance of food – look what we throw into garbage dumps – you're going to eat a lot. If you have less income and less availability of food, most likely you're still going to eat all you can get your hands on, but it's just not available.

Looking at the above statistics and thinking about the income and availability of food, think about this question: How common are garbage disposals in U.S. household kitchens and how many do you think there are in Haiti?

Now we'll take a look at the BMI – Body Mass Index – here in the U.S. First, understand that the BMI is a measurement that is calculated by entering your height and weight into a calculator and hitting "enter" and it gives you a ratio of your fat and muscle along with the other stuff in your body – mostly it tells you about fat. Your BMI is not the percent of fat you have in your body.

It's also helpful to understand what's "underweight," "normal," "overweight" and "obese."

Underweight	BMI	less than 18.5
Normal	BMI	18.5 to 24.9
Overweight	BMI	25.0 to 29.9
Obese	BMI	over 30.0

According to the CDC (Center for Disease Control) obesity contributes to heart disease, liver disease, sleep apnea, stroke, type 2 diabetes, some cancers and depression among other medical issues. The cost of obesity in the U.S. for additional medical bills is $147 billion a year. On the average, each obese person spends $1,429 a year on medical bills than the average person.

The CDC reports the following percentages of obesity by ethnic groups:

Blacks	49.5%
Mexican Americans	40.4%
Hispanics generally	39.1%
Whites	34.3%

74.1% of the people in the U.S. were overweight (this includes the obese) in 2007 and it has gone up since then.

There have been studies that have tried to give modern learned reasons for over eating and most all make some degree of sense. They say we over eat for many of the following reasons: to be social, to relax/escape/decompress, just simply mindless eating without realizing what we're doing, some get a "rush/high" from eating and some just eat from habit and some for comfort. These miss the point: it's that thing way down inside our DNA (instinct?) that says Eat When It's Available.

It seems that only the auto industry is bigger than the weight loss industry. There's always a new weight loss program. Weight loss companies spend millions advertising. There are hundreds of weight loss books on every theory you can imagine and then some.

As a doctor friend once told me, if there was any diet that really worked in the long run, there wouldn't be all these books and programs. He told me that weight loss is very simple: calories in, calories out. If you take in less calories than you use up, you lose weight – if you take in more calories than you use up, you gain weight. Simple.

* * * * * * *

Earlier in this chapter we talked about the root of the various "vores" with them all being from the Latin "vorare" meaning "to devour." A very closely related Latin word is "gluttire" – meaning to "gulp down" is almost the same, but with a broader context. Gluttier can mean not to just over eat, but to over indulge in just about anything. Here's where we can tie this to our favorite demographic – politicians.

Who devours or gulps down more of everything than a politician? From my perspective, not even the Tiger Shark or the Caterpillar. They can't get enough money in the campaign chest, can't get enough TV time, their name in the paper or on the internet. They are compulsive about being seen with all the right people – just let a higher ranking politician come into the area or a celebrity and you're going to see their face in the shot.

The devour/indulge in anything and everything that is going to make them more of a household word – sometimes to their detriment as we saw much earlier. They all want to do something meaningful so they add to laws and regulations that only destroy individual freedom and individual responsibility.

When it comes to anything that looks like it is going to increase their notoriety, it's like a feeding frenzy for politicians – their display on the evening news is watching starving pigs being thrown a bucket of slop. That instinct that most humans can keep under control simply does not exist with politicians. Let me know when you've seen one who has passed up an opportunity for a favorable moment in the spotlight.

CHAPTER V

SAVE FOR A RAINY DAY

EVEN IN THE SAHARA? "Save for a Rainy Day" for some reason this reminds me of when I heard somebody say (or maybe I read it): "They say a stitch in time saves nine, so they take a thousand stitches today to save nine tomorrow." Maybe that was in a U.S. government publication – the taking a thousand stitches part.

Having began each of these chapters with the animal kingdom version of the topic, I'll do the same here, however it will be much shorter in this chapter as this idea of "Save for a Rainy Day" seems to be pretty much a uniquely human trait/instinct. There are a few animals that have this sort of irrational behavior.

Perhaps a bit more definition is needed to have a clear understanding of just what behavior I'm critical of with "Save for a Rainy Day." There is nothing wrong with setting aside something for you when that particular something may not be available.

A couple of for instances of what is reasonable as to saving for a scarce time:

A savings account at a bank or an investment account to assure that if one has a sudden unexpected need for funds, or if one's source of funds disappears without warning, a reserve of funds will be available.

Emergency supplies and equipment. Should there be a power outage or the road washes out and you happen to live in an area which is remote and without easy access it's wise to have emergency supplies and equipment. For instance some people put away several gallons of fresh water, fuel for heat, maintain a gas-powered electric generator and have non-perishable food supplies set aside.

The examples above are but two wise plans regarding "Save for a Rainy Day." That's not what this chapter is about. Here, as with all prior chapters we are discussing the irrational extremes. For this chapter we'll go with: *The extreme accumulation of anything beyond any reasonable justification.* Some may refer to such activity as *an insatiable desire to accumulate possessions* – of any type.

But first, our animal friends. Unlike the animals in Chapter IV, Eat When It's Available, here we talk about those who don't just put away food they're not going to eat until another time – which is usually good planning – we talk about those who accumulate what they are not going to possibly need:

Magpies: They have been known to accumulate such things as money, jewelry or anything shiny. Magpies may have quite a digestive system; however I don't believe they are going to receive much nourishment from these various non-edible items.

Ravens: Another that accumulates any shiny object they can get into their nest.

Rodents: These will generally bring back to their resting areas most anything they can carry regardless of if it's shiny or edible.

Cats: Anybody who has had a cat for a pet, or known others with pet cats, know that cats will collect most anything they can hall away and hide. Most of the time, you'll find the toys their owners have given them hidden away, but there will be other objects also. Visiting recent friends who have a cat, she found the cat had hidden away a pack of Skittles, a bottle cap and also the lens cap from one of her cameras.

Dogs: Much as cats above, you'll find dogs accumulating things that they can't eat or do anything more than merely play with. But, just try to take one of these objects away from them – you'll give up the contest for fear of pulling their teeth out.

* * * * * * *

This is a trait where humans excel. While when we think about it, we understand that it makes little sense to accumulate beyond all practical use for what is gathered, we will – at time – admire the trait. The "Save for a Rainy Day" is often presented in a very socially acceptable manner.

In each of the following examples we are speaking of one person who has gone beyond all reasonable bounds regarding the accumulation of something in particular. Depending upon your own particular area of interest – or interests – you'll find one or more quite acceptable:

A personal library, mostly of first edition books and rare books, of more than 10,000 volumes.

Individual worth of a billion or more dollars.

More than three personal residences.

Stamp or coin collection with a value of more than $10 million.

Jewels with a value of more than $10 million.

Owning more than 10 personal vehicles.

Owning more than 5 personal aircraft.

An original art collection with a value of more than $100 million.

A personal wardrobe with a value of more than $10 million.

Owning more than 64,000 acres (100 square miles).

Having a collection of more than 10,000 DVDs – maybe that one's OK.

Having more than 4 wives – you deserve what you get with this one.

The last two are tongue-in-cheek and many of the above are OK for those who have been very fortunate and who have earned all they have through their own lawful hard work, lawful risk taking and inventive brilliance. I begrudge no level of success no matter how spectacular as to those who have earned it. I do not believe in income re-distribution.

To refine the concept of "Save for a Rainy Day" as presented in this chapter, are those who are driven to acquire more and more regardless of who they harm in doing so and regardless of what laws they break in doing so.

The classic example of the person I refer to is Charles Dickens' Ebenezer Scrooge in *A Christmas Carol*. We also have the comic book version in Donald Duck's Uncle Scrooge McDuck who was a stereo-type miser that loved to go in his money room and roll around in all his cash – in later stories he became a more benevolent fellow.

When you give it some thought, you'll realize that you know people who are very much in the "Save for a Rainy Day" category. A person need not have a lot of wealth to qualify. I know of at least one person who I've known for many years that will pinch a penny until it becomes a dime. This person will do anything possible to not spend a cent that is not absolutely necessary. I can't complain about one trait of cutting one's own hair as I do that myself – with not much more than just the one hair to cut, I see no reason to go to a barber.

Some such people may have much more money than they could ever expect to come close to spending, but will not enjoy the fruits of their lifetime labors. They are compelled not to spend money. Some even have no children to pass on their considerable wealth, but they continue to accumulate. Often they don't even have a passion for a particular charity, but will name one in a will just to have control over what happens to their money. Their fortune keeps growing and they become less able – mentally and physically – to enjoy life each year.

* * * * * * *

A sad example of accumulating beyond what a person can ever obtain any real benefit from is compulsive shopping and hoarding. These two often, but not always, go together. Among the worst examples of such activity are those who hoard animals. We see these in the news on occasion; the woman with the 39 cats, the man with a house full of dogs, and when we see these on the news the animals are suffering from malnutrition, injuries and various diseases – most of such animals have to be euthanized.

In practicing domestic relations law for many years, I've seen in more than one divorce, the occasion where one of the parties was a compulsive shopper and hoarder. In one extreme case, the photos of the interior of the home – about a 2,000 square foot three bedroom home – there was an accumulation of years of compulsive shopping and hording.

In the divorce case just mentioned, the photos showed a narrow path through the rooms – all the rooms – just wide enough for one person to walk. The floors in the paths were not always completely visible. There were stacks of boxes, packages, cloth goods and unidentifiable objects stacked from floor to ceiling throughout the entire home – except for the paths.

* * * * * *

And now to our favorite miscreants – the politicians. What is it that they crave, can't get enough of, have an insatiable desire to gain more and more of? That, dear friend is the easiest answer to any question raised in this book. I'll give the answer anyway, just in case one reader some place just arrived from spending his or her entire life out of contact with all of humanity and without the benefit of ever having read a book or had a conversation. The answer: POWER

To paraphrase Lord Acton "Power corrupts, absolute power corrupts absolutely." Many have repeated the phrase, and some others have even taken credit for it, but it was Lord Acton who first said it in the late 1800s. Power is something that politicians never seem to get enough of.

The one notable exception of politicians' insatiable quest for power that comes to mind – being an exception, perhaps he should not be considered a politician, but merely an office-holder – is George Washington. Following the conclusion of the Revolutionary War, many wanted General Washington to become King or even Emperor – he could have written his own title. Instead, he went to the Continental Congress, resigned his commission and went home to his farm.

Throughout history, from Biblical times to present we have the insatiable quest for power. Among the most notable was Octavian who, after defeating Mark Antony and Cleopatra, resulting in the unification of the Roman Empire acquired a new name: Caesar Augustus – roughly meaning emperor worthy of worship. He was referred to with many of the phrases we are familiar with as referring to Jesus Christ: Son of God, light of the world, maker of peace on Earth, born of a virgin, etc.

The Roman Emperor most recalled as a megalomaniac of course was Caligula. Many of Rome's absolute rulers did demonstrate what absolute power could do to a person who had the quest.

In more recent times we've seen the likes of Hitler, Stalin, Pol Pot, Idi Amin and most recently Kim Jong Un. These are those who either were or are without limit to their evil and were or are able to act without any restraint. We have others today throughout the world who fit nicely into the megalomania category however if I start throwing out names, I'll run into political divisiveness inappropriate to getting across the point herein. Thankfully, most of those who fit the category presently are not able to act without restraint.

CHAPTER VI

LET 'EM KNOW HOW YOU FEEL

GROWL, HISS, SQUEAL. No that's not your spouse, your neighbor or the guy that's rooting for the other team to win. Think back to the earlier comment about trying to take a bone or a piece of meat away from a hungry Pit Bull.

If you get too close to a Rattle Snake, it'll let you know. Most people have never come across an angry animal in the wild, but most have seen a dog letting you know that you're getting too close to its territory. If an animal is injured, it will also often let you know if you are getting too close.

Animals will make numerous different displays of anger, often also considered displays of domination. Among the mammals we see such things as:
Puffing-up: appearing as large as they can –
Primates will rise up to full height, pushing out their chest and spread their arms.

Noise: becoming as loud as they can. This can be a type of yell or roar.

Bearing teeth: this one almost everybody has seen.

Other displays: a ferret will make the hairs on its tale stick out to display what appears to be a much larger tail and we've also seen animals where the hair on the back of their neck will stick up.

Birds make interesting displays of anger:

Color: they can flash prominent color areas to warn that they are
angry.

Sound: they often will make a sound that is louder and different than either their usual communicating or mating cries.

Posture: some will stretch tall and others will crouch down as warning signs.

Attacks: as with other animals, birds will indeed attack. You have likely seen smaller birds attacking larger birds in the air if the larger bird has come too close to the smaller bird's nest.

Motion: some birds will move around such as slow side to side movements while keeping their eyes riveted on whatever other animal has gotten them angry.

Animal displays of anger are to protect themselves, their territory, their young or their food supply. Animals don't just decide it'd be fun to go out and harm or kill one another just for entertainment – that's left to that higher species – humans.

Unless you simply never read, listen to or watch the news on you've heard of dog fighting that's a spectator "sport" where dogs fight each other and a bunch of really sick pukes bet on which dog is going to survive the fight. Or you've heard of the same activity with cock fighting – same quality of spectators.

I hope you're not asking what about these dogs and cocks? They're angry as it comes and will fight to the death. No. The criminals involved in these activities have trained the animals to fight like this. It is not something they do without having us "top of the food chain" really intelligent species train them to fight like this and put them in the pit to die.

* * * * * * *

From the above you should be able to tell by now that the title of this chapter, "Let 'em Know How You Feel," isn't about all that touchy-feely communication stuff. We're not talking about giving others a clear understanding of what we're feeling inside or of trying to understand their innermost feelings. We're discussing "telling" not "discussing."

From my misspent youth (not really but it kind of sounds neat here) I have seen very common displays of anger from others. The one that is kind of humorous (except for the participants) are the two guys that have had too much to drink and begin to argue – think that maybe there's a lady at the crux of the matter?

What the two guys don't know is that they've just moved a few rungs down the evolutionary ladder. Here's non-higher brain antics:

Standing as tall as they can.

Puffing out their chests.

Talking loud.

Lips pulled back showing more teeth – if they still have them.

Rapid breathing.

Rapid pulse.

Pupils contracting.

So, what does all this do for them? The rapid breathing with the upper chest area pumps adrenalin for combat and makes the blood oxygen rich for energy. Their eyes are focused to cut out peripheral distraction so they can concentrate on the enemy. Just like when you're anxious in the doctor's office making it hard for them to draw blood, their veins have drawn down from the surface of the skin to reduce the risk of serious bleeding from injury. The full height, puffed out chest and loud voice are to frighten the enemy. – Wow, these guys are good!

I left out an opinion comment from above, for which I have no resource reference whatsoever: Their I.Q.s have dropped 20 points. – Ready to go now. First they flail around on each other; usually causing superficial damage. When they're done, they get kicked out and go directly to jail or get stopped by the police on the way to wherever they headed, and then go to jail. I leave with the lady.

Not wanting to give them any significant recognition, I'll just mention by category a significant number of angry individuals. What's really a sad indictment of our society is that there's no way to know if this group is really angry or if they are just acting angry because so many people in our society not only approve, but seek out these people. They make very good livings at playing into our society's insatiable hunger for anger. You've likely figured it out what group this is: talk show hosts – of which I'll name none.

A very dangerous, and growing in instances, of how people let others know of their displeasure is "road rage." This one is among the most ridiculous. Whatever somebody does out there on the roadway that is ridiculous, aggravating or even stupid just isn't worth wrecking your vehicle, getting a traffic ticket, getting injured, going to jail and certainly not dying for.

If somebody in front of you stopped for a yellow light that you think they should have gone through – so

you could illegally have gone through as it turned red –
that's going to add a whole minute to your trip. Wow, a
minute! If the two of you are going to the same location
and had gotten through the light before him, when you got
to your destination, you couldn't get out of your car and
get to the door of the building before him in the one
minute you saved.

Better yet: you're stuck behind somebody doing
55mph and you want to do 60mph. Because of curves and
dips in the road, you're stuck behind him/her for 5 miles.
5 miles, that's forever when you're in your little world in
that driver's seat. That idiot in front of you just has no clue
how important you are and how much of a national
security emergency it is for you to get to your destination
as fast as possible. After forever – 5 miles – you finally get
around him and do your 60mph the rest of the way.

Regarding the 55mph versus 60mph for 5 miles in
the example just stated above; do you have any idea just
how much of your invaluable time you lost? 27 seconds!

Now that I live in the South, I notice much less road
rage. Around here when somebody does something on the
road way that would otherwise trigger road rage, people
just say something like, "Bless his heart, his mommy and
daddy probably didn't have very high IQs either."
Of course by now, with the automobile having been
around for over a century, we have some degree of "road
rage" in our DNA. What is the most universal device on an
automobile? It was standard on all vehicles before
windshield wipers, way before the radio and long before

anybody ever heard of seatbelts. Different countries have different standards for equipment, but this has always been there on everyone everywhere – the horn! Horns – from the old squeeze the rubber bulb to the blast of a truck's exhaust horn. Heck, we've even got them on bicycles! "Let 'em Know How You Feel!"

Let's think about the not so violent everyday ways in which we express displeasure; or at least in the ways that we see it expressed by others – after all this book isn't about any of us.

Start with the little kids; first gesture, sticking out their tongue. Next comes the scowl, scrunching up their face, folding their hands across their chest and stomping their feet. Of course there are the tantrums in the grocery stores and restaurants where you don't know if you want to kill them or their parents.

About the next gesture for anger that is learned is the one that last the rest of your life – *"The Finger."* This one seems to cut across genders and generations. It can, however, be a humorous and at times even an affectionate gesture. Most often it is a sign of at least displeasure if not outright rage. It's often accompanied by verbal exclamations. Frequently it is displayed from the safety of your vehicle or a very safe distance. I know of one individual who always uses it below the window level in the car.

Be very careful about hand gestures when traveling outside the U.S.

even those that are positive here are often highly insulting abroad. It's best to simply not use any hand gestures when traveling.

* * * * * * *

We'll not get into the physical violence here – jails and prisons are full of them. Human to human physical violence is not found elsewhere in the animal world. As is often said, "Man's inhumanity to man, is without limits."

The verbal assaults are somewhat different. One of the saddest areas of such verbal assault is in domestic relations. It is well known among those who work with the topic – and recognized by those who are observant, but not trained in the field – that people tend to be the most verbally abusive to those who are closest to them. They know they're safe, because they know their spouse (or other close person) will not physically harm them – there is a great deal of physical domestic violence, but here we're only discussing the verbal.

There's also the symbolic antagonism that people use to let their feelings be known. Neighbor to neighbor – as in noise (music or whatever) too early or too late, stacking trash near the property line, parking your car in front of their house or draining dirty water run-off into the neighbor's garden. One neighbor puts up a lawn sign for a candidate and another goes out and gets a sign for the opposition. Kids will be kids.

At the other end of the spectrum, some will give the "silent treatment" to express their anger or displeasure.

One that tends to really aggravate many is found common among teenage girls – the rolling of the eyes and head. That one is so silly I have difficulty taking it as a serious gesture of anything; but, it is an expression of one's feelings. It is more civil than using a gun anyway.

* * * * * * *

Of course we have to wrap up with the politicians – probably the most expert at letting people know how they feel. Or, rather, what they want their constituents to believe that they feel – after all, the most important thing to them is not the good of the country, it's getting elected. Now, it doesn't hurt the politician's feelings if how they feel happens to benefit the country so long as they get elected.

We see them on TV all the time letting us know how they feel about government benefits, taxes, foreign relations, education, etc. They always let us know what they feel about the politicians in the opposing party – they are the bad guys. Every problem we have as a country now, in the past and that we will have in the future is because those bad guys in the opposition party – always.

It's always fun to see the clips of them when they are caught off guard – when they don't know the camera is still on or that the microphone is still on. There was the famous clip of a U.S. President telling the Russian President that he'd have a lot more leeway to make deals after the election was over. Gee whiz, was that the president just throwing 320,000,000 Americans under the bus? How about the Congressman that threatened to throw a reporter off the balcony of the Capitol rotunda if he ever asked him a question again that caught him off guard? Don't we just have the finest people ever looking out for us in Washington, D.C.?

Politicians control the ultimate expression of "Let 'em Know How You Feel" – war! Of course they themselves never put life or limb at risk. They just bluster about patriotism and love of country and send others off to suffer, be maimed and die. Very few wars have ever meant anything in the long run when compared to the suffering of the combatants and non-combatants affected – the most obvious exceptions to that statement were the Battle of Actium, Battle of the Milvian Bridge, our Revolutionary War, Battle of Waterloo, our Civil War and World War II. Many may disagree with the Battle of Waterloo being on the list and others would add to the list, but it's my list. Of course the politicians rarely suffer so they're always up for a new game.

The late, Dr. Harold Rood of Claremont McKenna College stated that war is permanent to the human condition. In his book *Kingdoms of the Blind,* he discusses how democracies always return to their follies of the past that so nearly caused them to loose their life – we see much of that in this country at this time.

Brian T. Kennedy, President of Claremont Institute and a recognized expert on national defense, stated in a 2013 speech (along the lines of Dr. Rood's comments) that "citizens of free nations in peacetime do not historically think in such terms." He went on to say that "...the U.S. is increasingly and dangerously vulnerable, and our elected leaders appear oblivious."

We all know about the Boston Marathon terrorist bombing. Did you know that the next day there was a terrorist attack on a major power station in San Jose, California? They cut the underground fiber optic cables, disabling communications and security systems. Next they used high-powered rifles to assault the extra large transformer and cooling system. John Wellinghoff, Chair of the Federal Energy Regulatory Commission at the time, said it was the most significant domestic terrorism involving our electrical grid ever.

Let's hope we make it through the next round in spite of the politicians we keep electing.

CHAPTER VII

KEEPING UP WITH THE JONES'

"I'VE JUST GOT TO GET ONE OF THOSE – ONLY BETTER. Did you see what that rotten Dave Williamson's got parked in his driveway? He's got one of those new bright green dual bladed John Deere rider mowers with the steering handles and giant yellow grass basket on the back! I hope he wrecks it the first time he uses it."

It's kind of hard to think of where in the animal world we get the idea that we always have to be "Keeping up With the Jones'. It seems to be such a really unique human quality to not only want to have what others have, but the dark desire to have "Jones'" possession lost, stolen or destroyed. We're just so very nice, caring and special as a species – doesn't it just make you feel warm and fuzzy all over? We're just so very special.

There are some studies that indicate that dogs will, at times, demonstrate conduct that can be interpreted as wanting to have what another dog or other pet possesses. Dogs will even move in to receive attention if their owner is showing attention to another person. For example if my wife gives me a hug, her dog will come yelping, whining and jumping to receive attention from her – he wants what I have: her hugs and attention.

Similar conduct has been seen in primates. In various experiments, primates have been observed to demonstrate a desire for an object that another has been given. The conduct becomes more pronounced if there are several other primates that have all been given objects but the one has been deprived of receiving any such object.

Except for only mild demonstrations of desiring that which another has (object of activity) among dogs and primates – "Keeping up With the Jones'" is a uniquely human quality. That it is unique to humans does not speak well for humans as a species. Some may wish to argue that this quality is one which produces motivation; however, it is as destructive a propensity as any we have.

* * * * * * *

In thinking about "Keeping up With the Jones'" (from now on I'll just say "Jones'") we'll look at both the individual obsession and then go to the macro – the big picture. As to the individual, I really appreciate the way that Will Rogers stated it so succinctly:

> "They spend money that they don't have to buy things that they don't need in order to impress people they don't like."

That kind of says it short and sweet.

It is hard to argue that the compulsion isn't an integral part of the human condition when we see how widely recognized is the Jones' compulsion. Consider that there used to be cartoons, cartoon series, books from various countries, a 2009 movie and various TV series from as diverse places as Australia and Barbados – all with the Jones' title. Some are not as negative as others. Regardless of how absurd and destructive the conduct, never the less, we continue.

Some people will pick just a particular item, class of items, activities or anything else that strikes them as something important to them – to show the world, or their friends that they are just as good as, if not better than the Jones'.

One of the more ridiculous examples that we've all seen is the guy – almost always a guy – that has the shiny car with the big chrome wheels with really wide tires that have an extremely thin profile. The car has a sound system that registers on the Richter scale – three states away. And the exhaust system – you'd think it was a runaway three-trailer semi blasting up a mountain side.

He's got more money into the add-ons than he paid for the vehicle. Way more than his neighbors or friends have ever put into a car. However, where does he live? He lives in a run-down shack of about 400 square feet that should have been bulldozed long ago. But – man oh man; what a car!
Sadly some of these guys have wives (or girlfriends) and kids that have to get their meals on school programs and haven't seen a doctor since birth. But – man oh man; what a car!

"But Mom, Suzie's got 5 piercings in each ear, one on each nostril, two in her belly button and she's going to get her nipples pierced next week." The girl says with a pathetic whine and crocodile tears coming down her cheeks. Mom says: "Jenny, I told you – no piercings until you're in the third grade. I don't care that Suzie's already got all those for her 7th birthday." To which Jenny throws a tantrum, runs to her bedroom, turns her TV up loud and calls Suzie on her I-phone.

Regardless of what it is, we'll go to extremes to keep up with, and if possible, surpass the Jones'. The newer or bigger boat, the wilder brighter neon hair, the bigger house, the better more luxurious vacation, the bigger breast implant or the season tickets closer to the 50 yard line.

* * * * * * *

Just for fun, let's make a list of Jones items that we've personally seen up close, have heard of in and around our neighborhood, place of employment, or have at least personally heard of. Feel free to scribble in the margin with other instances:

At Home:

1. Putting in better landscaping.
2. A more striking paint job on the house.
3. Improving outdoor lighting.
4. More (in number and quality) of Christmas decorations.
5. New metal roof.
6. New windows and/or door. Shutters maybe?
7. Hire regular landscape service.
8. Hire house cleaner.
9. Remodel.
10. New(er) big(ger) vehicle.
11. Swimming pool – really getting someplace now.

At Work:

1. Getting that promotion.
2. New title if #1 didn't work out.
3. Bigger desk – with a name plate.
4. Bigger office – not shared.
5. Bigger office with bigger window.
6. Corner office.

7.   Your own secretary – better: "Administrative Assistant."

8.   Name on the door.

9.   Company credit card.

10.   Business travel and you keep the skymiles.

11.   Company car.

12.   First class seating on business travel.

Personal:

1.   New wardrobe.

2.   Better hair stylist.

3.   Facials, manicures, pedicures.

4.   Teeth whitening.

5.   Tanning.

6.   Gym membership – No, make that Fitness Center.

7.   Personal trainer.

8.   Country Club.

9.   Life member, live theatre and symphony.

10.   Large selection of formal evening wear.

11.   Engraved invitations for your parties.

12.   Apologized to the Governor for not making it to dinner.

13.   Private wine tasting tour in France.

14.   Didn't apologize to the President for not making it to dinner.

* * * * * * *

Try as one might to say that it is part of some sort of survival instinct, or gene, and that indeed it is common to the animal kingdom, there is a really dark side to it that is not found anywhere except in humans. The dark side was mentioned in the opening paragraph of this chapter. If you can't get one as good as the Jones' (or even better) then you want theirs to break, be stolen or somehow have them lose it. "If I can't have it, neither can you."

It is the more disgusting side of this ugly coin when people who know they can't match or beat the Jones' destroy that which the Jones' do have. The most common form of this activity is vandalism – the intentional defacing/destruction of the possessions of others.

However we have even seen those jealous of the Jones' relationships work to destroy that relationship. Be it gossip to destroy good reputations or the guy trying to get another guy's girlfriend; we see it both in life and in TV programs and movies. In the entertainment industry (radio before TV) there have been the "soaps" – they've made an industry of this going on a hundred years.

Another rung on this ladder of despicable conduct is the mainstay of those who recognize their place in society is that of a complete "loser." They take what belongs to others – plain old cheaper than cheap thieves, burglars, fraudsters, robbers and others of that ilk. The bottom of that bunch are those who take from their employer, the elderly and otherwise vulnerable and below them – lower than whale dung on the bottom of the ocean – those who steal from their family.

There was a time in England during what was called the "Bloody Code" when in 1815 there were 225 capital offenses. Steal anything worth more than 12 pence and they hang you. Cut down a tree – of any size – they hang you.

Many argue that the Bloody Code was not effective in reducing crime – mostly by the anti-capital punishment group – but there's no argument that it certainly cut down on recidivism.

Almost equally distasteful, are those if they ever exceed the Jones in any specific category, they go to all extremes to let you know. They will take every opportunity to demonstrate their superior position, in anything, to others – "rubbing it in." While such conduct is merely rude as opposed to some of the illegal activity stated above, it is none the less a sign of poor breeding and not the conduct of anybody I'll be inviting to dinner.

* * * * * *

With often horrid results we have the Jones' compulsion at the national level – run by, whom else, politicians. The worst of the instances results in war – or whatever currently PC name is in use: police action; forward projection of national interest, countering violent extremism, annexation, self-defense training, etc. – the dead are just as dead regardless of what it's called. Regardless of the name, it always results in the same thing; many die and are maimed – _except_ the politicians.

But alas, as they (whoever "they" are) used to say, we start out with the extreme (war) when the "Jones" of the politicians is at all levels and is destructive to the very duty to which they say (they swear) they will uphold and perform with the highest honor. I suppose that tells us something of the honor of politicians.

Each elected political office has a specific duty. The District Attorney does not do the job of the Mayor. The Mayor does not do the job of a U.S. Senator. The U.S. Senator does not do the job of a State Treasurer. The State Treasurer does not do the job of a County Commissioner. And so on and so on and so on.

Each person elected to office is sworn into office and takes an oath to uphold the laws on which the particular office is based and to perform the duties of that office.

All political offices have one thing in common – they were created to lookout for the welfare of the citizens served by such office. The single and most important job – no, the only job – of the elected official is to assure the welfare (not "welfare" as in handouts) of those who he/she serves through the office to which he/she has been elected.

If you believe all that, then you've either spent your life in the ivory tower profession of higher education, you're a philosophical idealist out of touch with the real world, all you do is watch soaps on TV every day, you're in a drug or alcohol induced stupor, or – heaven forbid – you're a politician!

The single objective, the one and only goal, the pinnacle principle, the ultimate concern, and the single focus of the politician to get elected – or re-elected!! It's not your welfare, not the good of the community nor the good of the country; the only thing that matters to a politician is getting elected or re-elected. Say anything, do anything, promise anything, just get elected.

Once in office then they can start managing the affairs of that office to which they were elected. Their first priority is to take care of those who gave him/her money for their campaign – the biggest contributors first of course. If the office has the power of appointment then those friends needing or wanting those positions must be taken care of also.

There is of course the show of public meetings. You know – that's where you and others of "the great unwashed" can come to a council, commission, committee, or whatever meeting and give them both written and verbal testimony about matters that concern you, your interests, that of you community and the general welfare of the public. All this becomes public record. You go away feeling you've done your part. They all smiled at you, some even asked a question or two.

There isn't, of course, any public meeting law that applies in people's homes for dinner and drinks, or out to dinner, or out on the golf course, etc. There isn't any public meeting law concerning the politician speaking with their staff, their attorneys, those individual meetings with somebody in the planning department, etc. No public meeting laws in the places where the decisions are made and friends/contributors are taken care of.

But you ask: "Where's the "Jones" part in all this?" It's the person who wants to take the office that is held by another. It's the politician wanting to move up from one office to another. It's being re-elected so that with seniority the committee positions are better and more powerful. It's those who help the person get elected so that they can move up in power over others who have influence.

CHAPTER VIII

WHERE HAVE I HEARD THIS BEFORE

SOMEHOW ALL THIS SOUNDS VAGUELY FAMILIAR. It seems that I've heard these negative traits discussed someplace previously. Let's see now, in these chapters we've had: I, Me, My: SEX – or – Survival of the Species; Never Do It the Hard Way; Eat When It's

Available; Save for a Rainy Day; Let 'em Know How You Feel; and, Keeping up With the Jones'.

OK, I guess that makes seven chapters about seven negative (some really, really bad) tendencies in politicians – well, in all of us. Is the fog starting to clear a bit? Seven sorts of bad conduct.

If you're not there yet, then we'll jump in the "way back machine" and go way back – about one-thousand, seven-hundred years or so. A monk in Eastern Europe named Evagrius Ponticus started the idea. Good old Evarius was followed monk John Cassian (sounds much more western) nearly a hundred years later. A couple of hundred years later, Pope Gregory started to really pin it down.

However, where it all became really broadly recognized and part of the almost everyday lexicon, was in about 1315 when Dante Alighieri included all this in his work: *The Divine Comedy.* Of course it originated with Paul's letter to the Galatians (chapter 5, versus15-23) written about two thousand years ago.

Yep, we've been reading about "The Seven Deadly Sins." In the chapter order they were presented we would have the following:

I	I, Me, My	**(Pride)**
II	SEX – or - Survival of the Species	**(Lust)**
III	Never Do It the Hard Way	**(Sloth)**

IV   Eat When It's Available
(Gluttony)

V   Save for a Rainy Day
(Avarice/Greed)

VI   Let 'em Know How You Feel
(Wrath)

VII   Keeping up With the Jones'   **(Envy)**

Sound familiar? Come on, you remember hearing about these. If you don't remember hearing them in church, you must at least recall hearing them in any one of several movies. I remember especially the closing of *The Devil's Advocate* where Al Pacino (as the Devil) traps a guy that you presume had learned his lesson, and Pacino says: "Ah, pride, my favorite sin."

Are these wonderful qualities we have all because a zillion years ago some lady ate an apple that she wasn't supposed to pick off a particular tree or is this just the way we're wired?

You certainly saw people you knew in the various chapters above and many, many more who you have heard of. The numbers of politicians of who you are aware, now and historically, you found all through the above chapters are legion.

There are many different definitions for each of the "Deadly Sins" found in the chapters above. The general definitions (again in the order of the chapters) which I used follow:

Pride: This is considered by many to be the foundation of all seven of the *Deadly Sins*. It may be the anchor for all of them without which the rest may not exist.

Pride is self-love; it is considering yourself (or wanting yourself) to be better than others. In its silliest form we see the people in the background of an event being covered by the news (or at a sporting event being televised) pushing, shoving, leaning, wearing ridiculous costumes, or whatever trying to get themselves on TV. With the advent of social media, we have everything from facebook postings to "selfies" being posted. All to gain attention to one's self.

People will take credit for that which they themselves did not accomplish – how often do we see this? We see people taking credit for the work of others in places of employment, certainly among politicians and even regarding inventions. Didn't we once have a high ranking elected official taking credit for inventing the internet?

"It's all about me. I'm the smartest, the brightest, the fastest, the strongest, the most beautiful, etc. My jokes are the funniest, my thoughts the most intellectual and jewelry the shiniest and most expensive. There simply are not enough superlatives to describe me and my accomplishments. Wow – I should run for election!"

A singer by the name of Mac Davis had a big hit record back in 1980 titled *It's Hard to be Humble* which you can watch and listen to on You Tube – it kind of says it in a fun way. Do you think perhaps it wouldn't have been such a big hit if there weren't so many who felt the same way?

Lust: An intense desire – usually defined as sexual in nature – a craving excessive beyond the norm or what would be considered a healthy interest. The intense, extreme desire ("need" to the subject person) can also have as its target money, power, fame and such. It is an insatiable appetite (need) for personal satisfaction, but impossible to ever be satisfied.

The compulsion is for more and more and when the usual no longer satisfies, then the need progresses into the unusual, the abnormal. We have all heard of extreme cases of sexual depravity in the news and read of it in history – particularly the habits of some of the Roman Emperors. No need to go into the sordid, sadistic details here. For those with a "need" to learn more, you are welcome to do your own research.

Sloth: "I could care less." OK, that pretty much does it for *Sloth* and we can move on to the next one. Just kidding of course, but if you had to define *Sloth* succinctly, that would pretty much cover it.

This characteristic can manifest itself in several different manners from merely failing to utilize your talents and abilities to being completely sluggish and lazy. Some people who are slothful are mistaken for being depressed which is a completely different matter. Depression is not a decision that one makes but is an emotional/mental condition which the sufferer cannot help.

The slothful person is one who frequently fails to meet obligations or to keep promises. A person with a passive aggressive personality (a quality of certain sociopaths) will agree with what another says or demands and then just does what they want. In the cases where the promise results in inaction, it is seen as slothful.

In the movie *Seven,* the person who was murdered and given the title of "Sloth" was one who was starved to death. The writer may have been thinking of the Bible phrase from 2 Thessalonians 3:10 "If anyone is not willing to work, let him not eat."

Sloth can be to the point of self destruction by not even bothering to take care of oneself. In Dante's *Purgatoriao* those who were slothful in life were required to run continuously as fast as they can forever.

We see this among our politicians constantly. The U.S. Congress at this time has an approval rating of 11%. That certainly isn't because they are working really, really hard and just making a mistake now and then. How many times do we see politicians at all levels off on vacation, "conferences" or any other excuse for a trip away in luxury – at our expense.

Gluttony: We don't have to look far to see examples of this one. It seems that every year there are more and more examples of those who "suffer" from this one. Some airlines are even starting to make provisions for special seating – with higher prices – for those that are in this portion of our population. It has become so common that many no longer see it as some sort of abnormal behavior.

As with the many of the others, this one also has a direct Biblical reference: Philippians 3:19 "…their god is their belly…" St. Thomas Aquinas even came up with six ways of indulging in Gluttony:

> Eating too soon
> Eating too expensively
> Eating too much
> Eating too eagerly
> Eating too daintily (I'm not sure how this fits.)
> Eating wildly

Gluttony also includes drinking. I would suppose that this would include all those who can't go through a day without a few "Big Gulps" or other giant size soft drinks. Of course most of us have seen the results of those who drink too much booze with resultant loss of health, job, family and financial assets.

Some stretch this trait out to the excessive desire for anything beyond what a person actually needs for survival

– I wouldn't go that far – it would include too many friends; and, in some respects myself.

And as for our politicians – in addition to rarely seeing a skinny one – what can be said? Not only do they spend a great deal of time at this dinner, that dinner, the other lunch, a "working" breakfast, but they also seem to have a gluttonous appetite for everything – especially power.

As you'll recall from Chapter IV earlier, Gluttony can reach to other conduct other than just eating and drinking. However, one must be careful in expanding Gluttony (no pun intended) to broadly (again, no pun intended) lest it begins to impinge on our next trait: Greed.

Greed: This one originally was titled "avarice" from the Latin "avarus" meaning "greedy" or "to crave." As we saw in Chapter V, it is the inordinate love for riches. It makes the accumulation of wealth and riches a goal in and of itself. It has nothing whatsoever to do with what is needed or which can be used.

The accumulation of objects, of possessions beyond one's need, can of course be seen as being responsible. There is nothing wrong with planning for the future be it retirement, children's education or for possible future medical contingencies. The accumulation is only a sign of greed when it becomes inordinate beyond all reason.

Even for those who cannot afford expensive possessions, we see people who hoard. People will shop on TV – there are stations dedicated to nothing but TV shopping. Others will shop on the internet and not just on Amazon, but on many other sites including those with questionable second hand merchandise.

Among the worst of those who accumulate (other than the politicians) are those who accumulate through criminal enterprises. Recently in the news there were scenes of the home of a drug lord in Central America. There were rooms of cash stacked up as one would see in a bank vault in a movie; more gold and jewels than in most jewelry stores.

As for our favorite demographic – the politicians – I need not elaborate on this one. You can sit back and think of enough examples to write your own book. Of course that's true of each of these traits. It's my job to merely get you to thinking in a particular direction.

Wrath: Of all the traits, this is the only one that is not necessarily associated with self-interest or with selfishness. Wrath can also be equated to "rage." It is a desire for vengeance. Wrath goes beyond "anger." Anger in a reasonable balance is normal. When anger goes beyond a reasonable balance as to its trigger, then you are into the realm of Wrath.

Many of us have seen in one Mob (Mafia/Gangsters/Crime Lords/etc.) or another, one of the more senior and reasonable mobsters saying something to the effect of: "Before you embark on a journey of revenge, first dig two graves." Credit will usually be given to the phrase as an old Sicilian saying. Nope, it's a Confucius saying. I just thought I'd throw that in.

Wrath is the actual, or desire to, wreak havoc or vengeance upon somebody far beyond that which would be deserved. An example would be if somebody threw a rotten tomato at a freshly washed and waxed car and the car owner beat the person who threw the tomato to death with a tire iron. That may seem an extreme example but such events do occur. One of the most common real life examples we hear much too often is the live-in boyfriend who shakes the girlfriend's baby to death. Did you just have a wrathful thought? Or, was your thought balanced?

The feeling of Wrath can continue, or return, long after the act has occurred; the person has been punished by the criminal justice system or even after the person is dead. It can manifest in even small ways such as impatience. Some extend the definition to self-destructive behavior such as drug abuse and even suicide.

Wrath to some extent can be a good thing. Recall back to Chapter I that all animals have an instinct, are hard wired, whatever term you wish for survival – individually and for the species. When the person, the tribe, the country, the species is challenged with death or extinction it may take all the Wrath that can be mustered to survive the challenge. Too much thought and not enough immediate action can lose the day – for eternity.

Can you remember a politician who never exhibited Wrath? Isn't that what we see in the news almost daily that is merely shrugged off as "party politics" or "campaign rhetoric"? As mentioned above as to Wrath continuing after the person who is the target of the wrathful feelings is gone, how often do you hear current administrations (at all levels of government) making vile statements concerning immediate and/or long-since gone predecessors?

Envy: In some respects, Envy is similar to Lust and Greed in that Envy is an insatiable desire, a compulsive behavior. Anything that another has that you deem to be better than what you have, you either want it, you want something better or at the very least, you do not want them to have it.

The "it" can be material or immaterial. For instance, a material object can be a new car or, as in Chapter VII, that new riding lawn mower. An example of immaterial is another's education: a doctorate degree for example, or a really great job with public recognition such as the president of the local bank who is also the president of the Chamber of Commerce.

Some attempt to draw a line between jealousy and Envy. As you read those that attempt to make the distinction, the line becomes very thin, fuzzy, gray and not in the least bit a straight line. In some definitions of Envy you'll find traits that another says is jealousy and vice versa.

Fairly uniform in the definitions however is that you only find the desire to destroy that which is the possession of the other person in definitions of Envy and not in definitions of jealousy.

Relating this to our favorite scoundrels, isn't this the nuts and bolts, the foundation of every campaign we see – ad nauseum?

CHAPTER IX

THE DEVIL MADE ME DO IT

I DON'T KNOW WHAT CAME OVER ME; I've never done anything like that before, I'd just never do such a thing, I can't believe I did that – The Devil Made Me Do It!!

Wrong! No! He/she/it/whatever – Lucifer/Devil/Satan/The Evil One – did not MAKE you do anything!!!

Let's move backwards from current to very long ago. At this time, in most "civilized" countries, people who commit heinous acts may be found to suffer from a mental "illness" of some sort – be insane? – and not understand that their act is destructive. They may not even be able to comprehend that there are such concepts as right and wrong. As horrid as their act may have been, they are not held responsible and are placed in a facility where they will no longer be able to hurt anybody. Did the Devil make them perform the act?

In some less "enlightened" countries, it doesn't take much to have committed a wrongful act and among those China would be #1 on the list with thousands of executions a year – the exact number is a state secret.

Iran is second in number of reported executions with 369 in 2013 and Iraq with 169 also in 2013. In many

Middle Eastern countries such as Iraq, Iran and Afghanistan the executions which are counted are only the formally sanctioned ones and do not include the village beheadings. These places are primarily theocracies and executions can be based on violation of theocratic law. Were all those who were executed made to do their deeds by the Devil?

It wasn't all that long ago, historically speaking, that even in the early days of on this continent there were witch trials and burnings at the stake. There was the frenzy of such trials that most of us had heard about in Colonial Massachusetts in about 1692-1693 when there were about 200 witch trials.

In the middle ages, there were the religious inquisitions under which uncounted numbers of people suffered torture and horrible deaths for violating Christian laws – as interpreted by men. Again, were all these people forced to do whatever deeds they did, or make omissions they should not have, by the Devil?

What of the Aztecs' human sacrifices around 500 to 1500 CE, before they even knew of Judea-Christian religion? They believed they were acting according to what they believed their god wanted. Was that the Devil?

Continuing back: the Celts' human sacrifices around 800 to 1 BCE? They certainly had no knowledge of the Judea-Christian Devil. They were acting according to their belief. Was that the Devil?

As mentioned earlier, is all evil because the Devil made some lady eat an apple off a tree she from which she wasn't supposed to eat?

TO CLARIFY MY PERSPECTIVE: I believe in God, the God of the Judea-Christian religion and that Jesus is the Messiah. I do <u>NOT</u> believe in Lucifer/Devil/Satan/Evil One.

I find no place in the Bible where the Devil created anything. I find no place in the Bible where the Devil forced anybody to do anything. Opportunities to conduct ourselves badly have always and will always exist. That we do them is our inability to control our subversion of our natural survival instincts – our automatic reactions. We have the brain capacity to change from what nature has given us – unlike the animals, but we just go with our base nature because it's easier and self-indulgent. The Devil didn't create temptation. He had nothing to do with creating anything.

* * * * * * *

Ah, but what about the story of Job you say. Recall that much of the Bible is symbolism, metaphor, numerology is common throughout and parables are everywhere. As just a bit of interesting background for purposes of thought understand the definitions of: *Parable, Fable* and *Fairy Tale.* All of these methods of story telling have one thing in common: they contain a lesson about life – how we should live, what we should or should not do and things of which to be wary. They all have a moral, a message. The differences in them are as follows:

Parable: The characters are human.
Fable: The characters are animals.
Fairy Tale: At least one character is a mystical creature.

The story of Job (the only place where it appears that the Devil actually <u>did</u> anything) is a *Fairy Tale* – the mystical character is the Devil. The story contains metaphorical imagery.

The message of Job, "the moral of the story" is threefold:

1. To understand that bad things do happen to good people. That's just life. That's how it is. Learn to live with it or find another planet.

2. Just because bad things happen to you, doesn't give you an excuse (or reason) to become a bad person. Being a good person is in itself reward enough. By continuing to be a good person, good will again come your way.

3. Live life to its fullest – according to the basic principles of God's Commandments – but to its fullest. Get out of it all there is to enjoy. Live it in

such a manner every week, every day, every minute.

In all these sort of stories, the events are not to be taken as historical fact. What is important however is the message they contain – and in that message, they are ultimately true!

I read in a book, some time ago, where the author was speaking about this topic of stories and meanings. In that book he wrote of an occasion where he was at a conference and a Native American lecturer began by saying something such as: "This is not the way it really happened, but it is a true story." The author went on to say that if you could wrap your mind around that comment, you had a very good chance of understanding the Bible.

We, the human race, have the greatest mental capacity of any creature on the Earth. However, we also have the absolute number one instinct/drive, or by whatever term you wish to give it, to survive. We have this trait on the individual level and will do anything to assure our survival. It's all about me: I, Me, My. All the other negative traits can be tied back to this one – the one that in the Seven Deadly Sins is called ***PRIDE***.

The End
Or
Forever?